THE ROYAL CRUISING CLUB

THE ROYAL
CRUISING CLUB

SEASON 1979
Published in the Centenary Year
1880~1980

Edited by
MALDWIN DRUMMOND

PRINTED FOR THE ROYAL CRUISING CLUB
London : 1980

Angus & Robertson · Publishers

London · Sydney · Melbourne · Singapore · Manila

First published in the United Kingdom by
Angus & Robertson (UK) Ltd. in 1980

Copyright © RCC Press Ltd. 1980

ISBN 0 207 95941 2

Printed and bound in Great Britain by
R. J. Acford Ltd., Industrial Estate, Chichester, Sussex

OFFICERS OF THE CLUB

MARCH 1979 TO MARCH 1980

Commodore . . . . DR. RONALD A. ANDREWS
Vice Commodore . . . . JOHN POWER
Rear Commodore . . . . W.H. BATTEN
Hon. Flag Officer . . . . JONATHAN TRAFFORD
Hon. Secretary . . . . EDWARD BOURNE
Hon. Treasurer . . . . EDWARD KENNERLEY
Foreign Port Information . . . . ANTHONY BUTLER
Hon. Librarian . . . . CHRISTOPHER BUCKLEY
Hon. Steward . . . . RICHARD COLEMAN
Hon. Solicitor . . . . PAUL KIMBER
Hon. Editor and Representative, RCC Press Ltd. . . . .
MALDWIN DRUMMOND
Crewing and Cadet Secretary . . . . KIT POWER

Committee

AIR CDRE. BRIAN MACNAMARA

BOYD CAMPBELL	M. HARVEY
GEOFFREY NOCKOLDS	TREVOR WILKINSON
LADY ROZELLE RAYNES	MICHAEL GILKES
J. VIRDEN	EWAN SOUTHBY-TAILYOUR

Assistant Secretary
MISS JANET PATTEN
33 HESTERCOMBE AVENUE,
LONDON SW6 5LL

Club Rooms
42 Half Moon Street, London W1

CONTENTS

LIST OF ILLUSTRATIONS

EDITORIAL
ACKNOWLEDGEMENTS

The Editor is grateful to members who took so much trouble in the writing and presentation of their logs.

The art of translating a log into a Journal was covered very ably last year by Ralph Hammond Innes. What at first seems to be a simple task soon becomes a labour and it is to the credit of this year's contributors that their work is clearly a labour of love. The Editor received 140,000 words and so it was just not possible to use everything so generously offered. Many of the logs that do not appear were of an unusually high standard and even include, regrettably, subsequent prize winners.

The charts this year were the work of Mrs. C. Wheeller, who has succeeded Aydua Scott Elliot, to whom the Club owes so much. The distinguished marine artist David Cobb, a member of the Royal Cruising Club created the little sketches of life afloat.

Nick Parsons of Angus & Robertson spent many hours on the book and the Editor is particularly grateful to him and also to the Managing Director of the company, David Harris.

Finally, the Editor would like to express his gratitude to Dick Stower of Laurent Giles for his information on *Vixen* and to R.M. Bowker and Group Captain F.C. Griffiths for their permission to use photographs of *Dulcibella* ex *Vixen* in the former's excellent edition of *The Riddle of the Sands*. He is also in debt to Stanford Maritime and Hugh and Robin Popham for their help and their photograph of *Vixen* in the Solent in 1899. The Editor's task would have been far more difficult if it had not been for the enthusiastic help of the proofreaders and he would like to include them in his thanks.

Message from the Commodore of the Royal Cruising Club:

THE ROYAL CRUISING CLUB TODAY 1880-1980

At the time of our Golden Jubilee our Commodore Sir Arthur Underhill wrote these words, 'I would express my most urgent hope that if, when another fifty years have elapsed, the Club is still in existence, it will be as friendly, as happy and as useful an institution as it is at present.' I think that we can justly claim that at our Centenary we still represent these qualities and remain a society of friends as our founders intended. In 1980 by accepting membership of the Royal Cruising Club a candidate still undertakes to mix with his fellow members when they meet afloat.

It is only by preserving this heritage that we can hope to keep the joy and satisfaction we experience at times when cruising, moments when time for once becomes an ally, when realities are clear cut, when this spinning and tumultuous world of today sleeps on its axis, and when we too can still find that inner peace which is itself freedom.

Dr. R.A. ANDREWS
Commodore

MESSAGE FROM THE COMMODORE OF THE CRUISING CLUB OF AMERICA

The members of the Cruising Club of America join me in saluting the Royal Cruising Club on the occasion of their centenary.

In its hundred years, the RCC has set an example for everyone, certainly for our club, founded by people who felt the lack on our side of the water of something resembling the RCC.

Indeed, it seems to me that the attitudes and values pioneered by the RCC will find adherents wherever people cruise. They will want to explore as well as to return again and again to familiar places. They will want to go out of their way to help others who propose to venture on to the sea. They will enjoy the cycle of engagement with the sea, followed by recurring companionship at the end of the day or the voyage. They will mark this companionship with story or song or simply with a mutual appreciation of the things that surround them; and they will look over, test out and in due course, accept those advances in the art that serve to make their cruising safer or more enjoyable while managing to avoid the paths leading to technological excess.

The CCA is happy to have a membership that is dedicated to closely related pursuits. One would be hard put to find some significant difference in outlook or basic values. True, our historic involvement with ocean racing puts a modest tax on our cruising time for some of us, but we pursue this at a measured pace and without expansionary aims. It is also true that much racing today seems to be moving in philosophical directions that give us concern – and we wonder what will have become of this facet of the CCA when it too comes to observe its centenary.

In this latter connection, we look forward eagerly to celebrating it with our good friends of the RCC, and note that we have only forty-odd years to go. Meanwhile, good sailing to you all.

R.C. McCURDY
Commodore

iv

THE CHALLENGE CUPS

Awarded by The Vice-Commodore, John Power

The Challenge Cups have always seemed to me to be one of the Club's pleasant and cherished anomalies. Surely the very nature of cruising is to get away from the pressures of competition, and all the tension, deceit and doublethink that goes with it; yet here we are competing with each other for the best cruise. Surely the best cruise is the cruise that gives the greatest enjoyment to those taking part, not just at the time but with hindsight afterwards, and yet noewhere in the rules for the Challenge Cups is the judge directed to take this into consideration. One of the hallmarks of the Club is the value that we set on unsung achievements; with the cups, however, we reward the blower of the loudest trumpet.

With this in mind your judge has interpreted the rules fairly loosely in the hope that he has observed the *spirit* of the competition more accurately than the letter. Indeed, as is usually the case, the majority of logs submitted were deficient in one respect or another according to the rules, and several arrived for judging after 30th November, with the result that certain cup winners may find their logs omitted from the *Journal*. This year, therefore, your judge has retaliated by introducing his own rules, too. For instance, he has disqualified from the competition a member whose otherwise excellent log describes an incident involving undoubtedly bad seamanship and bad manners in a foreign port; he has awarded marks against another who is known to have carried out his cruise under the burgee of another club, believing that the merits of the cruise will be recognised by the club concerned; and he has allowed his cup of coffee to spill over the words 'not for competition' where, in his opinion, the words were not underlined sufficiently to indicate that the author really meant it. If, in doing so he has failed to interpret the wishes of the membership as a whole, he apologises; but not for the matter of manners. Our Club sets itself on a pedestal and as such is an Aunt Sally for people to throw tomatoes at. Bad manners, let alone bad seamanship, can only damage our Club and are therefore unforgivable.

A total of thirteen cruises were considered for competition, of which seven fall into the category of 'shorter cruises'; one other, that of Venetia Hayward in *Robertson's Golly*, was a little difficult to place. Her total distance was 3,578 miles, placing her firmly in the 'longer cruise' bracket, and in fact beaten by only one other. The total length was forty days, somewhere between 'shorter' and 'longer'. The log is in fact of a short North Britanny cruise and a separate cross-Channel trip to Cherbourg in April, followed by two sails around the Atlantic, the first qualifying for the two-handed 1981 transatlantic race and the second to the Azores and back single-handed. Perhaps a little harshly, I decided that although these could perfectly properly be taken into account in the competition, cruises involve making ports of call and the total of only ten ports visited established the log as a 'shorter cruise', which nevertheless I enjoyed reading. Total use of the engine was only 1.1 per cent, and even if the race and qualifying cruise are excluded, the figure was only 8.7 per cent which was high laudable.

Of the other 'shorter' cruises, *Fair Joanda* went to Connemara after Tom Fenwick had cleverly arranged a business call in County Cork on the way. I would be interested to know what travelling expenses his Tax Inspector allowed him for the voyage there. Fourteen ports were visited in nineteen days of pretty dreary weather before the boat was left in the Kenmore River. Andrew O'Grady and his wife Sally took *Harkaway* a 21ft. LOA boat with only 5ft. beam, to the Channel Isles and Lezardrieux. Although I have no doubt that her owner would loyally defend her reputation, the reader is given the impression that *Harkaway* gave her owners a few problems, all of which were overcome with resourcefulness and no effect on morale. The sand over soft mud at La Chambre, Ile Brehat, is a sinister trap for anyone using legs, and they were lucky there was no substantial damage. The engine was used only 10.5 per cent of the time, perhaps because life was easier without it. This is nonetheless a low figure for a cruise in strong tides with little time available.

In *Felicity Al*, a 6-ton sloop, carrying Squadron Leader George Glenn and his wife Elaine, set off from Dartmouth for Britanny on 5th June, after a three-day delay caused by forecasts of fog and was then beaten back by a head wind. The next day they tried again and made Salcombe, where they were joined by their son, David. The subsequent trip across the Channel resulted in an arrival off the Britanny coast in thick fog, and I admired the way *Felicity Al*'s crew followed the seamanlike course of settling down to the long trip round Ushant to the west of the shipping lanes instead of returning to England or, worse, trying to grope their way in among the rocks of L'Abervrach. The essence of the Club's type of cruising seems to me to be found in a readiness to alter plans and remain at sea in order to attain one's objective in a safe, seamanlike manner. The trip from Salcombe to Benodet took fifty-six hours and the cruise continued as originally planned; *Felicity Al* reached the Vilaine and returned to Dartmouth after eighteen days during which the engine was used 11.8 per cent of the time. I felt this was a well executed cruise.

Christopher Lawrence-Jones and his wife Gail sent in a beautifully presented account of their nineteen-day cruise in the Channel Isles in

Clairvoyance, a Voyager 35, during June and July. They visited almost every imaginable Channel Isle, not excluding Les Ecrehous and the Minquiers, as well as the coast of Brittany between St. Malo and the Trieux River. Furthermore, the log includes some excellent photographs and useful port information. The engine was used as much as 35 per cent of the time, but this is the price one must pay for rock-dodging in light weather and big tides.

Matawa works hard for her living, and 1979 found her on the north coast of Spain, where John Fischel and his family picked her up in Santander and brought her home via La Rochelle and the South Brittany coast. This was a cruise carried out by a strong crew, but time was against them and their resources were fully tested when gearbox failure in La Rochelle resulted in the rest of the cruise being undertaken under sail alone. To add spice to the occasion, the Fastnet weather, with its associated period of lesser gales, passed through while *Matawa* was battling her way north and west against the clock. There was perhaps more enjoyment in recanting adventures after the event than there was at the time; however, I gained the impression that morale remained high. *Matawa's* safe arrival home at Dartmouth crowned a substantial achievement of which her crew can be proud. The engine, perforce, was used 6 per cent of the time, 672 miles were covered and thirteen ports visited in three weeks.

Harry and Pam Senior went with a friend through the canals to South Brittany in *Palafox II* and returned to Dartmouth along the north coast. The trip must have been a harrowing one, as they had already decided to sell *Palafox* in view of the arthritis that had stricken them both. Apart from the canal trip, the engine was used for a creditable 26.4 per cent of the time, and the log contains much information, particularly on the canal.

From two people who are thinking of swallowing the anchor, we move to someone who has just begun to cruise. At the age of 160 days, Jane Virden joined *Sharavoge*, newly arrived in Crosshaven from Plymouth, and sailed with her parents, Jonathan and Joy, in the cruise-in-company and subsequently up to Dingle, from where *Sharavoge* was sailed home by another crew. Although cruising with children creates problems, these problems vary with the age of the child concerned and do not necessarily decrease as the age of the child increases. However, I can think of few less compatible mixtures than a tiny child, a Folkboat and a cruise-in-company. Jane was to be seen taking a prominent part in all of the varied parties.

Of the six 'longer cruises', Jim Bourne collected *Janet Mor* from the yard at Goteborg, where she had wintered and, early in the season, sailed single-handed to Flensburg. Here he was joined by the first of a number of crews who, with him, sailed *Janet Mor* north to Trønsberg in Norway and then round the south and west coasts of Norway to Kviturspollen and then to Fair Isle, a passage of forty-six hours. From

Fair Isle they went south to Inverness, then through the Caledonian Canal and the Clyde to the Isle of Man and Ireland, where contact was made with the joint cruise-in-company at Castletownshend. After a short cruise in the Kenmare River, Jim left Union Hall, again single-handed, for Falmouth where *Janet Mor* found the best berth during the Cowes Week gale – on her legs on the beach by the RCYC. Here she was seen to be flying her Q flag in great comfort, while others fought the elements in the harbour. This magnificent cruise, lasting ninety-four days, during which no less than seventy-two ports were visited and 2,596 miles covered, ended in Dartmouth. Over a thousand miles were sailed single-handed and the engine was used 41 per cent of the time.

Water Music III returned home from the Adriatic via the Ionian Islands, Sicily, Gibraltar and La Coruna. This was a meticulously executed, well-crewed cruise in two parts; the first part was in May, after which the boat was left in Corfu until July, when the passage home began. This log is of the high standard to which we have become accustomed from John Foot. Almost everything seems to have gone like clockwork, and when it did not, there were reserves of resource and ingenuity available to overcome all difficulties. *Water Music* is a fine powerful ship and as in previous years, John made the most of her capabilities.

Keith Holland–Gems submitted a mammoth tome which, on inspection, turned out to be an account of the doings of *Scalza* during the years 1977 to 1979; therefore the final year was considered as an entry for the competition. *Scalza* was collected early in June from Frioul near Marseilles in the most appalling conditions. After herculean cleaning, she sailed single-handed to Sete where she entered the Canal du Midi. Dick Bishop, her co-owner, joined at Marseilles and there followed a delightful trip through the canal. *Scalza* then made her way up the west coast of France, finally making a passage from Camaret to the Yealm. Apart from the canal, the engine was used for only 23.7 per cent of the time, which I consider to be low for a boat as small as a Contessa 26.

Ralph and Ursula Fisher found themselves singing a hymn in church one morning which, if the tune is half as good as the words, should become the Club's anthem. It reminded me of the philosophy of *pereginare pro Christo* which spurred St. Brendan and his fellow Celtic monks into astonishing voyages in the ninth and tenth centuries. Ralph and Ursula circumnavigated Ireland in *Yeong*, a 30ft. junk-rigged Kingfisher, experiencing some very indifferent weather and making calls at several extremely adventurous places, including Castletownshend, where *Yeong* met up with the cruise-in-company. The combined ages of her two crew amounted to 150. Only people of Ralph and Ursula's experience could have overcome the problems involved, so this astonishing statistic was an asset rather than a liability.

Thirty-seven ports were visited in fifty-three days and although the engine was used 33.9 per cent of the time, this was fully justified by the exploration carried out.

It takes a good deal to deflect *Saecwen* from her purpose, but she met her match in the supreme Soviet of the USSR. On the rebound, as it were, she sailed south and in a superb 98-day cruise, visited ports throughout Spain and Portugal, Gibraltar and Spanish Morocco, returning to Lymington on 5th October after covering 2,927 miles and visiting thirty-seven ports, some of them more than once. The combination ages of the three crew on the voyage outward to Gibraltar amounted to no less than 212, and this trio of ancient mariners made a series of fine passages, one of them — from Bayona to Cascais — without use of the engine. The log records a lot of valuable information. *Saecwen* visited M'diq and Ceuta in Morocco, as well as making the trip up the Guadalquivir river to Seville.

There is news from Bayona of *Hunza's* departure on another of her unsung single-handed express transatalantic voyages and like many before, *Saecwen* arrived off Plymouth in bad visibility and unable to raise a squeak from the Eddystone radio beacon. Incidentally, Trinity House has now finally admitted failure with this beacon and plan to resite it ashore.

When it came to awarding the cups, I had considerable difficulty. I felt that almost all the cruises submitted were, in their various ways, well up to the standard we expect. I hope that others share my belief that we should not take our cups too seriously, because if I was really vigorously attacked I should have difficulty in defending my decision to withhold an award from several of the logs submitted. Eventually I made up my mind and the awards are, therefore, as follows:

The RCC Challenge Cup	:	Captain Colin McMullen in *Saecwen*
The Romola Challenge Cup	:	Rear Admiral R.L. Fisher in *Yeong*
The Founder's Cup	:	John Fischel in *Matawa*
The Claymore Challenge Cup	:	Squadron Leader George Glenn in *Felicity Al*
The Sea Laughter Trophy	:	Andrew O'Grady in *Harkaway*

TELEGRAM AND TINTACKS

by Maldwin Drummond

The telegram from Flensburg read: Delighted: please bring a number 3 Rippingille stove – signed Davies. Replies of this sort, from short-handed yacht owners, must have travelled the wires of the world countless times over the last hundred years. This particular message may have been fictional, for it was part of the fine web that came from the imagination and pen of Erskine Childers in his classic *The Riddle of the Sands*, first published in May 1903.

The instruction 'bring a number 3 Rippingille stove' persuaded Carruthers, a gentleman used to yachting with a capital Y, to go to the East End of London to purchase 'a formidable and hideous piece of ironmongery' for Davies. He had to transport that and a good deal else by cab and Flushing steamer to join *Dulcibella*. The telegram and the story that followed captured the fibre of many a landsman and led him, like a diving gannet, to deep water.

The only other small-boat sailor to achieve so much with his pen was the American single-handed navigator, Captain Joshua Slocum, who published his experiences in *Sailing Alone Around the World* in 1900. He describes how he discouraged the Araucanian indians from trespassing aboard *Spray* by sprinkling tintacks on the deck. The two books, published within three years of each other, turned many eyes seawards and, together, perhaps did more than any other publications to turn two nations into yachtsmen.

The heroines of both books have long since disappeared. *Vixen* was broken up at Lymington at the end of the war, having lain derelict for many years in Wootton Creek. The 35ft. sloop *Spray* was lost at sea. Joshua Slocum had set out in November 1909 on another lone voyage but was never heard of again.

Many replicas of *Spray* have been built and her lines are comparatively well known; *Vixen* is different, and a mystery as thick as a sea fret obscures her beginnings, even if her end is known. Perhaps this is as it should be, for the sub-title of *The Riddle of the Sands* is 'A Record of a Secret Agent'.

Childers bought her in 1897 and recorded in his log (which still survives): 'The *Vixen* was bought in Dover on Aug. 1 and fitted out for cruising in the Granville dock.' Erskine Childers had been elected to the Royal Cruising Club in 1893 and he had owned first *Shulah* and

1

then *Marguarite*, whose accommodation was a 'bell tent of oiled canvas'.

Hugh and Robin Popham, in their very readable and carefully researched account *A Thirst for the Sea* (published by Stamford Maritime, 1979), which makes use of many of Childers' surviving logs, record how he wrote to Walter Runciman from *Vixen* in Sonderburg, 'But did I ever tell you I had got another one?' The 'other one' was *Vixen* and that is where the puzzle begins.

The first and perhaps most important point to make, especially to those who keep a copy of *The Riddle of the Sands* in the yacht's bookcase and have read it many times, is that the fictional *Dulcibella* need not have the same vital statistics as *Vixen*. There is no doubt though that the wild days behind the Dutch and German Frisian Islands, recorded in *Vixen's* log from 11th August to 16th December 1897 during her voyage from England to the Baltic and back to Terschelling, unerringly found their way into the pages of 'The Riddle'.

Much has been written about *Vixen* and it is worth trying to sift the evidence yet again in an attempt to discover her true identity. It is necessary to look first at her vital statistics, particularly the draught, and then to speculate on what sort of lifeboat parentage she may have enjoyed.

To begin with, look at what Childers himself said about his new yacht. His contribution to the Royal Cruising Club *Journal* of 1897 was entitled 'To the Baltic, Through the Frisian Islands' and he says, 'Our own boat was an ex-lifeboat, cutter rigged, drawing 4', without the plate and by the help of small bilge-keels, sitting almost upright when on the ground.'

The *Yachting Monthly* magazine published his experiences in more extended form in Vol. 1 No. 3 of April 1898. In 'How We Drifted to the Baltic in a Seven Tonner', he said: 'She is a cutter, 30' over all by 7, drawing 4', or 6'6" with centre plate lowered. Her ballast is 3 tons of lead, carried inside in small pigs.' Childers repeats the information about the bilge keels earlier in the article when he 'leads' the reader below. He remarks: 'In the "saloon" he would find but just enough headroom to allow him to sit upright and before he could help himself the observation would escape him that the centre plate case was an inconveniently large piece of furniture.'

Erskine Childers, then of 20 Carlyle Mansions, Cheyne Walk, London, registered *Vixen* at Southampton on 16th August 1899, two years after he had bought her. The Register records that *Vixen* was a sailing boat, built at Albion Road, Ramsgate, in 1893 by J. Price; her official number was 110259. She was a cutter, with a semi-elliptic stern and a straight stem, carvel built and of composite construction. Her statistics were as follows:

Length from fore-part of stem under bowsprit to the aft-side of the head of the stern post	28.05ft.
Main breadth outside of plank	7.6ft.
Depth in hold from tonnage deck to ceiling at midships	3.08ft.
Depth from top of beam amidships to top of keel	3.78ft.
Depth from top of deck at side amidships to bottom of keel	4.05ft.

These figures are similar, although not exactly the same as the measurements published in a profile and deck plan of *Vixen* published in *Yachting Monthly* in March 1945 and accompanying a letter from H. Hanson of the Cruising Association. *Vixen* was now renamed *Dulcibella* in honour of the book and was lying at Lymington. The *Yachting Monthly* plans and the particularly fine photographs, taken by Group Captain F.C. Griffiths in 1942, that appear in R.M. Bowker's *Unique Edition of the Riddle of the Sands* are clearly of the same vessel, *Vixen* later *Dulcibella*. It is surely the same yacht pictured in the Solent in 1899 (see photographs) and borrowed from Hugh and Robin Popham's excellent book on Childers' sailing career, *A Thirst for the Sea*.

The draught measurement is worth noting, for in the *Yachting Monthly* profiles it is 2ft. forward and 2ft. 9ins. aft. The peculiar counter, according again to the profile of 1945, added 3ft. 3 ins. to her 28ft. (28ft. 5ins. according to the Register), making *Vixen* 31ft. 3 ins. overall, from the foreside of the stem to the supposed outside of the counter (it had partially rotted away by then).

As has been noted, Childers records his *Vixen* as an ex-lifeboat of 30ft. overall, with a beam of 7ft. and a draught of 4ft. with the plate up and 6ft. 6ins. with it down. The differences between Childers' figures and those recorded later, as far as overall length and beam are concerned, are small. Yachtsmen recording their experiences in the Royal Cruising Club *Journal* and *Roving Commissions* are seldom very accurate when it comes to telling of the vital statistics of their craft and often round up such measurements. This cannot explain, however, the great difference in the draught measurement. Childers definitely states 4ft. and he had been sailing in waters where an exact knowledge of a yacht's draught was essential. Indeed, in *The Yachting Monthly* in 1898, he re-emphasizes his yacht's draught: 'A light draught is indispensable of course; ours of 4', is I should think, nearly the maximum for comfort, though the channel is navigated by small traders, loaded down to as much as 7'.'

This is a definite statement and it is difficult to believe that there is any lack of precision in it. He can hardly mean something less than 4ft., say 3ft. 9ins. The discrepancy, therefore, is 1ft. 3ins. It is certainly a puzzle.

3

On the 1945 drawing, the measurement from the bottom of keel to deck amidships is shown as 3ft. 10ins. and in the Register this is given as 4.05ft. The three tons of ballast plus all the books and other equipment meant that she was heavily laden and perhaps well down on her marks. Later this was further exaggerated by brother Henry who, according to the log, 'brought loads of guns, cartridges and big new double oil stove, and our fine old *Shulah*'s [his first yacht] compass'. (This was no doubt the origin of the telegram in *The Riddle of the Sands*.) With all this extra load and bearing in mind Childers' remark in the *Yachting Monthly* article *Vixen* had 'a low freeboard, a high coach-house cabin roof, and a certain over sparred appearance aloft, that would unnerve the most honied tongue', she would have sunk if encouraged to a 4ft. draught.

What is the explanation? Hanson, in his letter to the editor of *The Yachting Monthly* in March 1945, is convinced – principally because of this draught measurement – that there were two *Vixen*s: the first with a draught of 4ft., in which he did the epic cruise in 1897, and the second surviving to show a less extravagant demand for water until broken up in Lymington after the Second World War. In order to support this theory he claims, without giving sources, 'Belgian Yachtsmen emphatically assert on evidence of eye witnesses, that *Vixen* was lost on the return from Terschelling in 1898.' R.M. Bowker, in his edition of 'The Riddle' comes to the same conclusion. The actual log, however, disproves this and although the cruise home was undertaken in poor visibility, Childers (helped by Alfred Rice, a Burnham yacht hand) successfully collected her from her winter quarters and took her safely to Dover. She was laid up at Moody's yard, at Burseldon on the Hamble river, by the middle of August 1898. The 1899 log covers the period from 30th March to 30th April, cruising only in the Solent and returning to Burseldon. The photograph '*Vixen* in the Solent 1899' was probably taken during this time. There was therefore only one *Vixen* up to May 1899 and, most likely, she became *Dulcibella* in both fact and fiction.

What was the answer then? If she were the same boat, how could there be such a discrepancy in draught? A possible answer is a small false keel, for it was fairly common to increase the windward ability of a lifeboat conversion by adding to the keelson. To ensure that *Vixen* sat 'almost upright when on the ground', small bilge keels would have been needed and he recalls these in the *Yachting Monthly* article mentioned above. After Childers' experience behind the Frisian Islands in 1897, it would have been natural for him to have removed the false keel and shortened the bilge keels.

To turn to the other principal question: what sort of lifeboat conversion was *Vixen*? There are obviously two candidates: a Royal National Lifeboat Institution conversion and an adaptation of a ship's lifeboat. Erskine Childers had sold *Vixen* in 1900 for £12, according to R.M. Bowker, and he seemingly swallowed the anchor for two years until he bought the 15-ton yawl *Sunbeam* (formerly *Zephyr*) in 1902. *Vixen* became the houseboat of George Newbury of Sarisbury Green, 'Hillary' – or Claude – Hapgood bought *Dulcibella* in the early 1930s. He was both a yachting journalist and the owner of a small boatyard at Fishbourne on the Isle of Wight. He records, this time in *The Yachting World* of 26th May 1933, that his new acquisition *Dulcibella* 'was originally a 30′ life-boat, double ender, diagonally planked in teak'. He continues: 'Whoever would have the pluck to put a counter on a pointed stern?' He illustrates the point with a photograph of the old boat on the slip at Fishbourne, his head and shoulders appearing from a central hatch in the coach-roof. The aft 'addition' gives no clue to the parentage of *Vixen*, but it is worth trying to suggest an answer to Hapgood's question.

The Register records that *Vixen* was built at Ramsgate by J. Price and had an 'elliptic stern', a phrase that covers almost any form of counter. The Ramsgate beach boats, in common with other Kent-shore fishing craft, sported a development of the lute stern, which gave extra space for working and for stowing nets. The design also improved the boats' beaching and launching performance. The advantage of this type of stern would have been known locally and a builder, faced with creating an 'elliptic stern' out of a diagonally planked hull, would no doubt have achieved it by adding further fore and aft planks and then drawing them out aft to form a counter, thus increasing valuable space on deck. Group Captain Griffiths' photographs show the diagonal teak construction and the additional fore and aft planking on top.

Dick Stower of Laurent Giles, a relative of Claude Hapgood, knew *Vixen/Dulcibella* well when she was in the Wootton yard and is an authority on the yacht. In his article, 'The Riddle of *Dulcibella* – Some Thoughts on an Old Boat', he discusses the photograph in Claude Hapgood's old *Yachting World* article: 'Her hull was an easily driven type, typical of the old rowing lifeboats, and in no way like the ugly boxy modern ships' lifeboats which are poor sailers, depending on radio telegraphy rather than sails for salvation.' He felt certain that *Vixen* was originally an RNLI lifeboat. In an article he published in *The Yachting World* in 1979 he recalls the progress of his very successful re-creation of *Dulcibella* for the recent excellent film of *The Riddle of the Sands* produced by Drummond Challis's company Worldmark Productions Ltd. In this, Stower is clear that the fictional *Dulcibella* was also an RNLI conversion. *Dulcibella* he writes, 'as everyone knows, was a converted RNLI rowing lifeboat.' He took the Brook 35ft. rowing lifeboat *Susan Ashley* as the basis of his *Dulcibella*. *Susan Ashley* was built in 1907 and served at Brook on the back of the Wight until 1935, when the station closed. She was for many years under the charge of Coxswain Major General Jack Seely, later Lord Mottistone and sometime Secretary of State for War. The lifeboat

Susan Ashley saved eight people from the Norwegian barque *Souvenir* in February 1916 and, in February 1917, five from the ketch *Mienje*. She made a very photogenic centrepiece to the film and provided a further boost to the idea that *Vixen* had been also an RNLI conversion. Graham Farr, a noted authority on RNLI boats, discusses her identity in 'The Riddle of *Vixen*', a contribution to a newsletter of the RNLI Lifeboat Enthusiasts' Society. He identifies her as the *Vixen* that appears in Lloyd's and was built as an RNLI boat by Forrestt & Son in 1866. Forrestt was a well known Institution lifeboat builder. In Lloyd's Register, this yacht is shown with an overall length of 33ft., which is too long, although just possible; but the inflated beam of 10ft. 5ins. and a Thames tonnage of thirteen, rather than eleven seems to rule her out as Childers' *Vixen*.

The present Registrar at Customs House, Southampton, puts a further obstacle in the way of this identification, for he is reasonably certain that a vessel recorded in the Register as built by J. Price of Albion Road, Ramsgate, would have been built there. If she had been converted to a yacht by that firm, the Register would show it; but it is silent on the subject.

If *Vixen* was built by Price in 1893 as a lifeboat and converted either by them or someone else in the four years between 1893 and 1897, when Childers bought her, she could hardly have been in the RNLI fleet, as it is unlikely she would have been sold out of service after so short a time. Mr. Linklater, who is responsible for launching-records at the RNLI at Poole, could find no trace of Price building any lifeboats for the RNLI. Lloyd's Register shows that he only built one other yacht, the 6-ton cutter *Pet* in 1888. She was 25ft. with a breadth of 7.2ft. and a draught of 3.5ft; coincidentally *Pet* was registered in the Port of Southampton as was *Vixen*.

The Griffiths' photographs show the double-diagonal construction clearly and the handsome materials indicate an RNLI conversion rather than some other form of lifeboat. *Vixen* has the look of a small Norfolk and Suffolk type boat, with a flatter sheer than was customary in the more common James Peake self-righting boat, which became the mainstay of the RNLI fleet.

It is time now to take an opinion from the late George Naish; he was Deputy Director of the National Maritime Museum, Honorary Secretary of the Society for Nautical Research and a member of the Royal Cruising Club. In correspondence with David Cobb, the celebrated marine artist and member of the RCC, he says: 'She lay on the mud for years in the Hamble River – I never thought of her as a lifeboat – but I may well be wrong.' Later he sent a picture of *Dulcibella* with a note: 'As an RNLI lifeboat she wasn't; – much less sheer.'

Ted Watson, who bought the Wootton Yard and the near derelict *Vixen/Dulcibella* from Claude Hapgood, agrees and writes: 'She struck me rather as an old ship's lifeboat rather than one built for the RNLI.'

Double-diagonal construction was used for ships' lifeboats. Some of Fitzroy's special boats on HMS *Beagle* were of an early form of that construction and they proved particularly tight after long periods out of the water. Ship's lifeboats tended to be of standard lengths too — 28ft., 30ft., and so on — two feet being added to allow more survivors to be carried. Could *Vixen*, therefore, have been a 28ft. ship's lifeboat, built on spec perhaps by Price or — remembering her quality — as a special order and then finished off by him as a yacht, making use of well known local techniques for adding the counter?

Childers could not have added the counter, for he only took ten days to fit her out after he became her owner in Dover on 1st August 1897. It *is* known that he reduced her rig. Dick Stower says that it took a remarkably short eight weeks for Tim Bungay to convert the RNLI lifeboat *Susan Ashley* into the film *Dulcibella*, including the addition of the counter and, with Harry Spencer's help, the provision of the masts and the rigging.

And so the riddle of *Vixen* is still with us. It may never be unravelled or understood, just like the famous telegram that started this investigation. Kit Power of the RCC remembers sending exactly the same message to his crew as a joke when cruising in the area in 1957. The poor crewman had never read *The Riddle of the Sands* and so spent hours searching the East End of London for such 'a formidable and hideous piece of ironmongery' before joining; but unlike Carruthers (Davies' crew for *Dulcibella*) he was unsuccessful.

A LAST-MINUTE CRUISE:
Sailing and Climbing on Scotland's West Coast

by Robin Knox-Johnston

Suhaili was due to go on semi-permanent exhibition at Brighton this year but, in June, when the masts were unstepped and the rigging coiled and greased for the journey south, these plans were cancelled. Until this cancellation, I do not think that I had fully realised how little my heart was in the Brighton business; the moment I heard that she was not going south, I felt an inexpressable lift of spirits and immediately began to plan a sail as a celebration.

We moved up to Scotland in 1978, sailing *Suhaili* round in the early Autumn. Apart from the odd visit to Barra every four years in the Round Britain Race, everything north of the Clyde was unknown to us and as soon as we knew that we had a boat available, we decided to go and explore the islands of the Inner Hebrides and take a quick look at Barra if the weather was cooperative. We had no particular itinerary; we thought we would potter wherever our fancy took us, although this would inevitably mean downwind, as *Suhaili* does not like going to windward. Our crew consisted of Sue and myself, plus our daughter Sara and a school friend, Alison. Alison had to leave halfway through the voyage and we had to call in at Oban after our first week, so I arranged for Chris Bonnington to join in her place. We had been threatening to try out each other's sports for ages and the Cuillin Hills in Skye are not far from Oban.

We decided to sail in early August, which left us exactly five weeks in which to get *Suhaili* ready. Sue concentrated on the painting, I tackled the rigging and equipment and once Sara was home, she got on with the stores. The only job that did not get done was the engine overhaul, but as it was running all right I decided to leave well alone. I last overhauled it in 1974.

We sailed from Troon Marina at 0050 on 4th August, having been delayed for ten hours by a broken fan belt and the difficulty of finding a replacement. The wind was NW Force 2/3 and visibility excellent. Our course lay south of Arran, west to the Mull of Kintyre, then north up the Sound of Jura. We had a fine reach across the Firth of Clyde to Pladda, off the southern tip of Arran, which we passed at 0450, and Sue and Sara handed over to Alison and myself. The wind stayed about the same all night and as there was little fetch, we made reasonable progress until 0830, when it became calm. The visibility was quite incredible at dawn; we could see Rathlin, County Down, the Alloway peninsula and the heads of Ayr all at the same time. Sitting in the cockpit, having scrubbed the decks, with the smell of bacon and coffee wafting up from below where breakfast was on the go, I had that glorious feeling of well-being that one only gets sometimes at sea. It seemed a good omen for our cruise.

There is a pretty ferocious tide-race around the Mull of Kintyre, and as I wanted to have it going with us, I started the engine at 0830 and we took in all sail. Two hours later we were in the centre of the race, rolling the decks under and heading north with a light westerly wind. There were two other yachts in sight by this time, both inside, close inshore, carefully avoiding the race. We quickly left both of them behind and got a free deck wash into the bargain.

We had planned to make a brief stop during the day at Gigha Island, off the Kintyre peninsula. It had been particularly recommended for its clean white sandy beaches and its excellent cheese. We sailed into Ardminish Bay at 1430 and dropped anchor in twelve feet of water. A short jetty provided landing for the local launch ferry and we went ashore here to the post office, which was also the general store, and bought two large cheeses for £4.80 each. We thought about visiting the local gardens, but the wind was favourable and we decided to press on a bit further north before nightfall. It was only later, when I had time to read through a guide book to the island I had bought at the post office, that I discovered that Gigha had been King Haakon's base before the Battle of Largs in 1263, where he had suffered the major defeat which effectively finished Scandinavian rule in this part of Scotland. Although it seemed very quiet now, it had obviously been quite a thriving community then.

We anchored for the night in the small northward-facing bay on Eileen Mor, off Loch Sween. The Bay is small and we were the third boat in, about all the harbour would take. Even so, we all had lines out to anchors ashore to avoid swinging into each other – which was just as well, as the wind got up during the night. Last autumn Eileen Mor was bequeathed to the Scottish Nationalist Party in a will that ought to be challenged, so perhaps we were lucky to see it when we did. Like many places in the islands where Christianity had an early hold, Eileen Moor has the remains of an early chapel, roofless but well worth a visit and last used as an illicit still.

The wind was southerly Force 5 when we awoke on 5th August and as we wanted to go north, we felt in no need to hurry our departure. We weighed anchors at 1145 and having cleared the race off the entrance, headed up the Sound of Jura. Visibility was down to less than half a mile at times in misty rain, quite a contrast to the previous day, and after a short time, as we were able to make a comfortable five knots under this reduced sail area, I took in the mainsail and carried on under jib and mizzen. As we cleared Ruadh Sgeir we toyed with the idea of going through the Correyvrekan; the tide was favourable and an eight-knot tidal stream is too good to be ignored. Even on a calm day, you can hear the muted roar of the tide-race three miles away and the effect on the sea is noticeable for miles. However, we received a call from friends that they were awaiting us at Ardinamar, so we headed up the Shuna Sound instead.

Ardinamar, on the north-east corner of the island of Luing and presided over by the redoubtable Irene MacLachlan, is not an anchorage to miss. Its entrance seems all wrong; you leave Irene's two buoys to starboard, which makes the entrance channel seem very narrow but at low water the rocks from the island of Torsa reach right up to the buoys. The bay had ten yachts already at anchor (among them was *Shuna*, the boat we were looking for) and they were all anchored up under the hills to the west, so we sailed in and joined them. The evening was spent ship visiting.

On 6th August the forecasters warned of gales from the south veering NW rising from Force 6 to occasional Force 9, so we decided to stay where we were as Ardinamar is well sheltered. We went ashore and 'met Irene, looked through and signed her visitors' book, and discovered that she did not have much faith in the forecasters. She pooh-poohed my decision to stay put and, as each boat sailed from the anchorage, she turned to me with a twinkle and said 'There's another brave boat sailing then!' Nevertheless, I decided to stay where we were, and we spent the day walking over to Cullipool and exploring Torsa Island. As it happens, Irene was quite right about the weather, and if it blew more than Force 7 anywhere, there was no mention of it on the next forecast. That evening, the youngsters on the boats in the bay had a marshmallow toasting session ashore and we older people, who were not invited, got on with the more serious business of checking the flavours of various malt whiskies, apparently a west-coast pastime.

The forecasts for 7th August were just as baleful as the previous day, but we ignored them and sailed with *Shuna* and another boat for Puilladobhrain (pronounced 'Pulldorn'). We took the inside route through the Cuan Sound which, with a light headwind and five-knot favourable tide, gave us good sailing; and then we were out into the Firth of Lorne, with the Isle of Mull showing mistily about nine miles away to the west. Our course lay north-east though and on a reach, *Suhaili* overtook the other boats, only to lose the lead as the wind dropped. We tried to sail into this anchorage as well, but the wind died away completely, forcing us to 'donk' the last hundred yards. I cannot say the Puilladobhrain impressed me very much. It is not that well sheltered, the bottom is poor holding, the nearest pub is about a mile away, and apart from the Bridge over the Atlantic which is next to the pub anyway, there is not much to see. We spent some time exploring the creeks around the anchorage and burning the rubbish from a couple of boats. A light, but insistent rain began to fall towards evening, so we stayed on board and did some peggying. The anchorage filled up at dusk and by daybreak there were seventeen boats crowding it.

On 8th August it was agreed that *Shuna* would head straight for Dunstaffnage; meanwhile we would take a look at Loch Spelve and Oban and join them there in the evening. What a boon the VHF is: by setting set time we were able to check on each other's progress through the day and pass on any useful hints. We kept a regular schedule with *Shuna* at 1400 each day for most of the fortnight. The wind was SW Force 3/4 out in the Firth of Lorne, so we had romping reach across to Mull and the entrance of the loch. The entrance looks difficult on the chart but is easier than it appears. However, I had yet to find that out and with a contrary wind, we downed sail at the entrance and motored through the channel. Once inside the loch we had a choice of going north or south, about a mile or so either way. As we could not see what was round the corner to the north-west we headed that way and dropped the anchor in twelve feet of water. The holding was not good but with all 22 fathoms of chain out, our dragging was slow enough not to cause too much alarm when the squalls came down the hills.

We went ashore for fresh water from a stream and, finding it well sheltered and with a small pool beneath a waterfall, took the opportunity to have bracing showers. This is where we made the acquaintance of that scourge of the Hebrides, the midge; for some days afterwards we carried numerous bite marks as a memento of Loch Spelve. However, we did refill the watertanks with crystal-clear water as compensation; in fact throughout the cruise fresh stream water was readily available for little effort. Loch Spelve was attractive and there was only one other boat on it all the time we were there, so it may not be that well visited. For those who like mussels, there are beds of large ones which are easily accessible at low tide.

We reached across the Firth of Lorne again and then ran up the Sound of Kerrera to Oban. The obvious place to moor in Oban is alongside the fishing boats — if they will let you — but we found a pleasant sheltered spot in the south-east corner of the harbour for half an hour.

Dunstaffnage lies about six miles north of Oban. The harbour is dominated by a fine castle, and it must have been an attractive out-of-the-way place before the research station was built. Now it is crowded with boats and buildings reaching down to the shore. The only space left for visiting yachts is very deep, which makes for hard work weighing anchor. We sailed early in the morning, noting Dunstaffnage for a sheltered overnight alternative to Oban but nothing else. The bulk for the day was spent restocking in Oban which has most of a boat's requirements. We had to go across the harbour to obtain fuel, but it was cheap when we got it and despite the so-called fuel crisis, we could have had all we wanted. Alison left us to catch the early morning train south and Chris arrived at about 1600, having searched the waterfront for some time before finding our little corner. We cast off at 1645 and headed for the Sound of Mull, straight through an interesting tide-race off the entrance by Eilean Musdile. It was getting dark as we came up towards Loch Aline and the tide was turning against us, so I headed north and anchored close into the shore in Ardtornish Bay, a delightful spot, out of the tide and well sheltered from the north-east to south-west, with good water and fine walks.

We weighed at 0255 on 10th August and, as there was no wind, set off northwards under power. Tobermory was abeam two hours later and Ardnamurchan abeam by 0637. Eigg, Muck and Rhum were in sight all morning as we 'donked' up towards Skye. Twice, fed up with motoring, we tried to sail; but after wallowing for half an hour each time, the Birmingham mizzen was restarted. We were heading towards Loch Scavaig, a small anchorage in the south of Skye at the entrance to Loch Coruisk, a large and incredibly blue freshwater lake fed by streams from the Cuillin Hills and regrettably with no navigational access. Soay, Gavin Maxwell's island, was abeam just before 1100, and shortly afterwards we were throttled right down and creeping into Scavaig, keeping a sharp watch for the numerous rocks. The entrance is sixty yards wide, clear at low water, but best taken slowly at high water when the rocks on the west side are covered. We let go the anchor in the south-east corner, as recommended in the Clyde Cruising Club handbook, but moved farther into the centre of the bay almost immediately as it was much shallower than indicated. On two sides the anchorage is sheltered by the Cuillin Hills. On the east the Cuillins provide protection just beyond the outpourings of Loch Coruisk and to the south some small rocks provide shelter. The Clyde Cruising Club handbook warns of sudden squalls, so we put out the entire 22 fathoms of chain on the 35lb. CQR and two lines to ringbolts on the islets ashore. In addition, I put out everything else on board on to a 35lb. fisherman laid out to the north in case the wind changed. For a day all this seemed unnecessary overkill, but when it blew later on I would have been happier with double the weight of mooring.

After lunch at 1400, we broke up into two parties. Sue and Sara went in search of a good washing pool, while Chris took me to what I considered to be an unclimbable piece of sheer rock face, 250ft. high, and made me climb it as practice for our assault on the Cuillin range the next day. Chris described it as 'very severe' in mountaineers' parlance, or, in his words, 'thought-provoking'. To me it was 'bloody terrifying'.

Skye is renowned for its midges and the rumours of their voracity are not exaggerations. At anchor, however, we avoided most of them. Our entertainment was provided by a family of seagulls: the parent gulls were trying to push the two unwilling youngsters out into the world.

The 11th August dawned reasonably calm. The girls found an open boat that occasionally transports campers between Scavaig and Elgol and took a chance on it making a return journey. Chris and I set out to climb the ridge. Unfortunately, thick low cloud obscured our view at about 1,500ft. and from then on visibility in the mountains seldom exceeded two hundred feet. Our first crisis came on Sgurr Bubh Beag. We had passed beyond the summit when Chris, who was leading, said he had forgotten about the next bit, a minor matter of a 50ft. vertical drop. 'We'll have to abseil down this,' he said. I glanced nervously over his shoulder, took one look and decided this was no place to experiment with a new (to me) technique. We hung on to the top of the cliff arguing for a while, but as I was not prepared to try abseiling without practice, it was up to me to come up with an alternative. Eventually I put a bowline on a bight around my waist, the standing part through a caribineer hook, then back to make a boatswain's chair lowering hitch, and down I went. Chris was not at all happy; he had never seen this used on a mountain before but it seemed a lot safer to me than abseiling. After Chris had abseiled down to join me we continued our climb along the ridge and reached the peak, Sgurr Alasdair, at about 1700. After a short break we started back down to Tchearlaich, along the ridge, down the wrong ascent, back up again and then 3,000ft. all the way down again over boulders and later grass to the bottom. We then followed a route that took us along the whole length of Loch Coruisk and were back on board by 2130. We had covered about seventeen miles in the day, but it was one of the most stimulating days I had had for a long time. The girls got to Elgol, started drinking a cup of tea, heard that the boat would make one more trip to Scavaig and caught it just in time.

Sunday 12th August started out relatively quietly but quickly developed into a steady Force 5/6 with squalls of more than that. The spindrift coming through the entrance was landing on the beach a hundred yards to the north, so there was no way we could get out of the bay. We kept an anchor watch, observing our two shore-lines coming up bar tight, and occasionally re-adjusting our anti-chafe precautions. Chris looked more and more grave as the squalls built up in intensity, mainly I think because I warned him that if one of my lines went, we were going to have to use his climbing rope to hold us in position.

It was not until 1600 that the wind started to show signs of easing and we decided to start bringing in some of the warps in preparation for a dash through the gap. At 1640 the wind lulled and we hauled up the anchor. We went at full throttle for the entrance and arrived at the same time as a squall from the other direction. *Suhaili* staggered, but

Suhaili

ten tons takes a bit of stopping and we blasted through. Had the wind been greater we would probably have paid off one way or another and hit the rocks either side. Once clear, the wind started to ease and, before we had travelled three miles and were in the Sound of Soay, it had gone, and mist had reduced visibility to a cable.

I liked Scavaig (apart from worries about its holding), the scenery was spectacular, and it was deserted. The girls thought it was rather spooky and were not sorry to move on, although they found the waterfalls good for washing (all the streams we came across had beautifully clean soft water), and our tame seagulls provided amusement.

At 1730 Soay harbour was abeam; it has a dangerous entrance that requires a lot of water, but there was a large fishing boat inside so it could be entered safely. We headed on into thicker fog and I was taking echo-sounding readings to navigate when suddenly we moved out into a clear sky and excellent visibility. We were heading towards Rhum for the night, and were making slowish progress, when Sara called out that she could see a large blue ferry to the south, but a different colour to the Mac Braynes steamers. 'How many masts?' I asked. 'Three,' was the reply. There is only one boat with three masts that at a distance might be taken for a passenger ferry and, sure enough, there was its warship escort two miles west. We went over to be nosey, dipped our flag (which was acknowledged), refused an invitation to play deck hockey, and left the occupants to a well-deserved holiday. Later on we received an acknowledgement on the VHF for our loyal greetings.

We anchored at Loch Scresort, Rhum, at 2000. The next morning we went ashore to the local store which had very little to sell as the ferry had not been in for a couple of days. The only public phone was out of order; it is connected by short-wave radio with the mainland, and it seemed to be assumed that sooner or later someone on the mainland would notice and report the breakdown. In the meantime no one seemed unduly worried. Most of Rhum is now divided into wildlife zones and although we were tempted to go climbing, we decided to press on for Tobermory as Chris wanted to catch the ferry back to the mainland. We had a pleasant sail in light conditions and entered Tobermory harbour at 2000. The harbour was full as the glass was falling steadily, although the forecast was not too bad. We anchored close into the shore and went ashore for a good meal.

The next morning we went alongside and collected fuel in five-gallon containers from the suppliers near the jetty. Chris joined the 1030 ferry for Oban, by which time we were in the Sound of Mull sailing southwards. We were under jib and mizzen as the forecast was not good, the glass was down to 979, and there were news flashes about casualties in the Fastnet Race. We anchored in Ardtornish again at 1320 and had a lovely long walk ashore before returning on board for an early evening disturbed only by occasional severe squalls and an otter which came and swam around for a while.

On 15th August the glass was rising steadily, so we sailed early, deciding to head to Colonsay for the evening. We had a SW Force 2/4 all day and tacked out into the Firth of Lorne, past the Garvallachs, about three miles to seaward of the Corryvrecken (where the tide-race was still quite noticeable), and finally into Scalasaig. The CCC handbook says to moor to the south of the pier and put a line ashore onto a ringbolt. This we did, but it failed to satisfy the natives, who kept coming down and telling us that we were going to be in the way of the ferry. I began to wonder what size the ferry was; larger than *Ark Royal*? Eventually, at 2200, we got out and went round to Loch Sturrsneg, where we spent a pretty uncomfortable night. There is an inner harbour at Scalasaig and if you do not mind drying out, it is safe in there, but the outer harbour is *verboten*.

We did not hang about at all on 16th August and weighed anchor early, setting course for Gigha again via the Sound of Islay. There was rain and headwinds all day, but it was clear enough to see the raised beach on Jura. We reached Ardminish again at 1730 but an easterly wind Force 4/5 made the anchorage untenable, and we carried on to West Loch Tarbert for the night, meeting gusts of thirty-five knots on the way. After anchoring south-west of Dunmore with a spring on the anchor chain we examined the levels in the gin and whisky bottles and then turned in early. I had noticed that many of the yachts we had met put an angel down on their cables when at anchor so it had a better chance of holding. One of the lessons learned on the cruise was that a 35lb. CQR gave little security in many of the anchorages where the bottoms were very soft mud. As a result, I have decided to add a 50lb. angel to *Suhaili*'s outfit. West Loch Tarbert was a good firm anchorage, and we slept undisturbed, awakening to a beautifully peaceful dawn and the reflection of the trees reaching to either side of the boat. It was difficult to leave such a peaceful spot, but I was determined to call at Gigha again to restock with cheese and we also wanted to get round the Mull, so we had to drag ourselves away. Apart from pursuing a runaway cheese down a hill, our stay in Gigha was brief and uneventful. We think it merits a lengthy visit some time. About thirty seals watched us arrive and leave from a rock near the entrance, and this might well explain why we caught no fish in the Sound of Jura either coming or going.

After three days of easterlies, the forecast at last admitted that there might be some easterlies about; we immediately had a NW Force 4 all the way down to the Mull of Kintyre and blew out our original and venerable spinnaker in the process. As this sail helped bring us back from India in 1965/66 I shall repair it yet again; but it is getting a trifle tired.

We rounded the Mull just after 1500 and soon handed the main as we heeled decks under to a sharp katabatic wind blowing down from the cliffs. Fortunately it was a beam wind and we had a super sail until we were well clear of Sanda Isle and crossing towards Arran. This was our best day's sailing of the whole cruise but, even so, we ended with a beat into Lamlash, which must have had fifty boats at anchor.

As the 18th was our last day we were in no hurry to get underway. We eventually crept out at 1500 after visiting friends on another boat. The water was totally flat and a rich brown peaty colour, always a sign of heavy rain in the Firth of Clyde. We donked quietly home, investigating a number of 20ft. basking sharks on the way, one of which hit our bowsprit guys with its tail fin as it dived. Within two miles of Troon a 40ft. whale suddenly surfaced about three hundred yards away and blew. That was our last exciting incident. We berthed back in the marina just before 1900.

IRELAND: FIFTY YEARS ON
The cruise for which the Romola Cup was awarded

based on a log submitted by Ralph Fisher

I feel the winds of God to-day
To-day my sail I'll lift
Though heavy oft with drenching spray
And torn with many a rift.
If hope will light the breaking crest
And Christ my bark will use
I'll seek the seas at His behest
And brave another cruise.

Scottish Hymn 528, Jessie Adams
1863-1954

Ever since I took my boat to south-west Ireland in 1930 I had wanted to explore the west coast. Ursula and I (combined ages 150) had been wondering whether we were getting too old for cruising, but when we found ourselves singing the above hymn in the local kirk we were inspired to have a go, taking in the Irish Cruising Club Jubilee celebrations in Kerry in mid-July.

Yeong (Cantonese for kingfisher) is a bilge keel Kingfisher 30 with my own two-masted junk rig. Owing to the impossibility of spreaders the masts are necessarily unstayed; in order to give the foremast enough bury in the hull, I had to rake it forward. In each of the past two seasons we had wanted to go to West Ireland, but our auxiliary engine had been so unreliable that we did not venture to that rather wild coast. The deciding factor had been that the two of us cannot get the anchor quickly in strong wind without the help of an engine. This year we replaced our Volvo with a later model, which was used unstintingly and served us excellently. We also installed a small electric windlass.

We left our home port Tarbert, Loch Fyne on 13th June. After nights spent in Loch Ranza, Lamlash, and Campbeltown while getting the bugs out of engine and windlass, we passed the night of 18th June in the Sanda Island anchorage. The 19th started foggy and calm and we motored the fifteen miles to Ireland without seeing anything until Fair Head appeared ahead. At midday a light breeze from the south blew away the fog and, as it increased, gave us a fine sail to Portrush.

On 20th June there was little wind, and we motored most of the way to Glengad Head. From there we struck off — in visibility of about

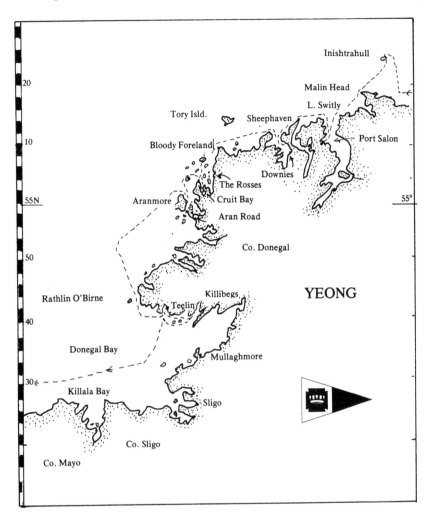

18

a mile – for Inishtrahull, where we crept into the steep-sided, narrow, rocky gut on the north side. This is about fifty feet wide and a cable in length and runs south-west into the heart of the island. We dropped our 7½kg. Bruce anchor to seaward and two young lighthouse men came down and took our stern warps to a little jetty on the south side. This rock-bound island is about a mile long and a quarter of a mile wide with a surprising area of cultivable land on top. Until 1928 it supported families with enough children to fill a school for forty; now there are only the lighthouse keepers who have no boat and are relieved by helicopter. It was a lovely still evening with many seals curiously investigating us; there was fog outside and the fog-horn booming on the hill. We walked round the island, rather saddened by the roofless crofts and school.

On 21st June we awoke to find the barometer falling, the wind fresh from south-west and predicted to become Force 6/8. We ran out a second stern warp on the port quarter to a ring in the rocks and felt very snug and smug: twenty feet on either side from the rocks and our stern thirty-five feet from the jetty. We spent the forenoon reading. At 1245 the inflatable dinghy landed on deck in a fierce squall and we spent an anxious afternoon wondering whether our small, doubled warp was chafing on the jetty edge; we went astern on the engine from time to time to relieve it. At 1600 a man came down from the lighthouse and, to our great relief, put on chafing gear and floated a stout sisal warp out to us. At high water at 1830 a bad swell began to come in and we ranged to and fro putting alarming jerks on the stern warps. The 1800 forecast for Malin was 'severe gale W Force 9'. In the evening the barograph flattened out and there was less wind, but a much worse swell began to come into the gut. At one moment there would be a three- or four-knot current surging in past the boat and about twenty seconds later a similar current running out. The inward surge dragged home our anchor and the boat started a to and fro movement of some thirty feet. In spite of putting the engine ahead each time to help check the sternway, we bumped our keels hard several times on a mid-channel submerged rock abreast the jetty. We were anxious, too, about getting the stern warps which periodically slackened caught round the propeller. We were busy until midnight trying to lay out better anchors, when both swell and wind finally subsided. We had had no lunch, tea or supper, only cocoa at 0100. Throughout the rest of the night we were restless and cold.

On 22nd June it was a quiet morning, but a further gale Force 9 was forecast for Malin. We debated leaving – but where could we go? Spring tides and a gale were not alluring. We decided to ride it out and laid out a 40lb. fisherman anchor to seaward, giving us a relatively anxiety-free night. The second gale never came and on 23rd June we decided to go. By the time we had recovered three warps and three anchors it was 1515. The Bruce anchor came up, embracing a

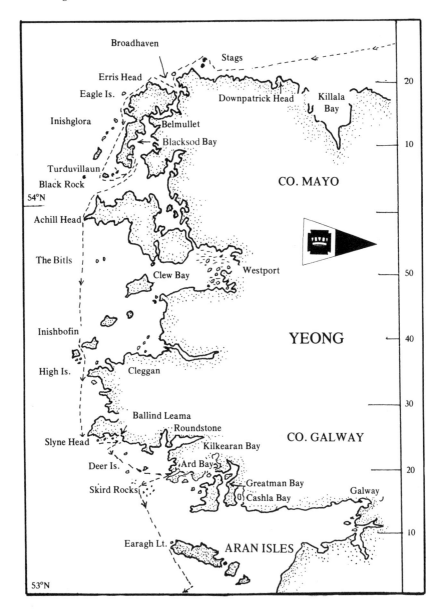

Broadhaven

Stags

Erris Head

Eagle Is.

Downpatrick Head   Killala
Bay

Inishglora

Belmullet

Blacksod Bay

CO. MAYO

Turduvillaun

Black Rock

54°N

Achill Head

The Bitls

Clew Bay   Westport

Inishbofin

YEONG

High Is.   Cleggan

Ballind Leama
Roundstone

Slyne Head   Kilkearan Bay   CO. GALWAY

Deer Is.   Ard Bay

Skird Rocks   Greatman Bay   Galway
Cashla Bay

Earagh Lt.   ARAN ISLES

53°N

20

10

50

40

30

20

10

stone the size and shape of a rugby football which made the anchor's three flukes quite ineffective. Furthermore, our faithful Danforth had one fluke bent so badly by strains that it was of dubious value. (This says something for *Fresh Breeze*'s old main sheet, part of which had been the warp pulling it.) I was amazed by the strength of modern cordage, which was demonstrated by the endurance of our very light running rigging, which has now remained rove in all weathers for five years.

We motored out and with a fine spring tide under us, shaped course for Malin Head. The lack of wind and the bad swell from north-west against the tide produced awful rolling. Everything below was a shambles. At 1930 we let go off Port Salon five miles up Lough Swilly on the west side. The wind was contrary, so the next day was devoted to various jobs, including changing the engine luboil. (Why do engine makers provide dip sticks of shiny steel which make it almost impossible to see the height of clean oil?)

On 25th June we made a slow beat westwards with engine, threading our way through a maze of unattended salmon nets off Fanad Head and finishing with a fast run under sail into Sheep Haven, where we berthed alongside Downies quay at 1530. The owner of the fishing boat *Mary Buchan* kindly drove me about two miles to get his cousin, a blacksmith, to bash our Danforth into shape. My tummy, which had been upset for the past day or two, was now better. This illness may have been caused by tasting the fluid in the engine-room bilge to determine whether it was oil, Bilgex, and salt water from the stern gland, or oil, Bilgex, and fresh water from our freshwater system.

On 26th June the barograph was high and steady with a north-westerly Force 3 wind, and we motor-beat all day past Tory Island. It was a sunny and not unpleasant journey, only rather tiring. After rounding Bloody Foreland, a significant milestone for us, we had a fast sail to Cruit Bay through the fascinating islets and rocks known as The Rosses and then anchored behind Odd Island. There is now a splendid little sheltered quay on the east side, abreast Odd Island, where we went alongside next day to post letters at Kincashla. Ireland had been without postal deliveries or telephones for eighteen weeks, but the postmistress shrugged her shoulders and said that it had not seemed to matter and the strike looked like ending soon.

The 28th June dawned overcast with wind west Force 3; but the sun came out and the wind seemed to be veering, so at 1215 we slipped and motored round Owey Island into a rather rough sea. The wind was now Force 5/6, so we decided not to plug on round Aranmore. Instead, we had an exhilarating run down Aran Sound to anchor in Aran Road at 1430. There were some fishing boats at the moorings, plus two small Irish yachts and the only RNLI lifeboat on this part of the coast. After we heard the gale warning, we let go two anchors.

The whole of the next day it was blowing Force 5/6, and we experienced some uncomfortable rolling. On 30th June the barometer was rising and the wind was NW Force 5. The two local yachts left and we followed suit at 1115. One of them had shouted that the south exit was too difficult and so we motored up to Aranmore Light into a beastly sea and swell. We stopped the engine at 1315 and found we could just lay the course for Erris Head, a distance of sixty-seven miles. With two panels down on fore and main we were making good progress; but the sky became overcast and menacing. We did not relish the thought of a night at sea, and altered course for Rathlin O'Byrne and Teelin, even though it added forty miles. Three times we were shooed round salmon nets by attendant boats. These nets and the incessant large swell are the curse of this coast. The nets – sometimes unattended – are one or two miles long with very small floats and are impossible to see at more than twenty yards. By keeping very close to the cliffs we managed to find the obscure entrance to Teelin and let go off the east pier. This cosy and beautiful inlet is well protected, but doubtless the squalls coming down off the 1,972ft. Slieve League must sometimes be horrible. However, we had a peaceful night with no swell.

On 1st July we lay in and had breakfast at 1115. The wind was now west. The day before, I had really known in my heart that we were foolish not to take the wind while it served to get us round Eagle Island. Heaven only knew when we would get a wind to take us out of Donegal Bay's deep indentation. When we were weighing anchor to shift berth a little, the windlass motor spun without turning the gipsy. I knew that a tiny screw must have come loose, but to put it right would involve dismantling the whole windlass on deck and we decided to run the ten miles up to the security of Killybegs and all the resources of that important fishing port. We weighed (with our hands) at 1340 and had a lovely run in sunlight with three panels down at six knots to Killybegs, where we let go in six feet between the quays at 1615. After tea I was able to fix the windlass myself. In Donegal, Mayo, and Connemara there is a delightful absence of officialdom.

The next day, we shopped for provisions and camping gas and weighed at 1240. We motor-beat down to St. John's Point and on to Teelin in a succession of rain squalls and negotiated a snare of salmon nets across the entrance. We let go in our old berth at 1600, turned in early and set the alarm for 0415.

On the 3rd at 0415 there was a flat calm and low cloud; we turned in again until the 0630 forecast. We weighed at 0640 and motored out. Visibility was quite good here but there was some obvious fog about. We shaped the course 225° to get in touch with the south shore, and with a visibility of one to three miles, we motored in calm as far as the Stags of Broadhaven (which we had to pass outside having found our way again barred by unattended salmon nets). Fog was coming in from Erris Head and after passing Kid Island, we were enveloped for a short time, but it cleared in time for us to identify Cashel Light where we anchored in the first bay past it on the starboard hand at 1930. It had been cold ever since Campbeltown and we had been wearing all our warmest clothes – and often oilskins as well; but this was a peaceful, secure anchorage on a lovely evening. We had much enjoyment from *Sailing Round Ireland* by Wallace Clark (Batsford) and also *The Armada in Ireland* by Niall Fallon (Stanford Maritime), which gives detailed accounts of the twenty or so Spanish ships wrecked on this coast (one of them half a mile from where we were now anchored). The wretched survivors of these ships were nearly all executed after interrogation.

On 4th July the wind was SSW Force 3/4 and there was no point in our battling against it. I rowed ashore to reconnoitre and found, just round the next corner, a fine new fish quay and a man willing to go up our masts to oil the halyard blocks. In the afternoon we motored round there and he did the job. He told us that that year the local open boats had been netting 150 to 170 salmon a night which they could sell to wholesalers in Belmullet for about £3,000. In Sheephaven, by contrast, they had been getting between only one and five salmon a night. It was a happy and successful day but we *did* need a wind with some north in it. We were held up for a further two days by strong head winds and we were getting anxious about reaching Southern Ireland in time for the meet. We finally left at 0645 on 7th July and, with the aid of the engine, reached painfully slowly towards Erris Head, only to be exasperatingly diverted about two miles to seaward by a boat attending a salmon net. At 1200 we rounded Eagle Island, another of our milestones, and stopped the engine. We had a nice afternoon's sail in a W Force 3 inside the Inishglora etc, intending to use Duvillaun Sound into Blacksod Bay. However, the visibility came down to one mile in drizzle and we thought it would be prudent to go outside all the Duvillauns. After having lost sight of all land, we finally ran the engine to make better speed in reducing visibility. We sighted Turduvillaun at half a mile and rounded it at 1640. We stopped the engine and had tea during a pleasant run in clear weather to Blacksod Point. We beat into Blacksod Quay and let go in two fathoms in the bay at 1820. We were eleven and a half miles as the crow flies from where we had started that morning. (How rotten of them to have stopped swinging the bridge at Belmullet!) There were lots of upturned curraghs on the beach. It was a quiet evening, overcast as usual, and – again as usual – we had to light the Tilly lamp to heat the cabin ... in July! We passed a pleasant evening playing chess.

The wind rose during the night and when the alarm woke us at 0630, it was SW Force 6 with rain. We stayed put. We had really putrid weather for almost the entire first three weeks. Gale, near gale, gale – we did not see the sun more than two or three times, and then only

Yeong

for short spells. When the wind had been at a suitable strength for sailing, it had been a head wind. There was more gloom when we discovered that I had left at home all our charts covering the Aran Isles round the south coast and up the Irish Sea. We were so despondent that we nearly decided to turn back.

The morning of 9th July was overcast with a NW Force 3. We weighed at 0830 and motor-beat slowly towards Achill Head, which we rounded at 1115 and stopped engine. The motion was horrible and I was seasick. We passed The Bills at 1250 and ran through Ship Sound to enter Inishbofin Harbour at 1810 and let go in the company of three small French yachts from the Centre Glenans base in Clew Bay. These were almost the first yachts we had seen since Portrush. The evening was calm and Inishbofin is a delightful anchorage. We had a further search for the missing folio of charts. We were out of luck, but we *did* find a 2424 'Valentia to Cork'. We decided that with this and the excellent plans in the wonderful Irish Cruising Club book, we could try to get to Castletownshend in time to join the cruise-in-company. As for getting home, we could see what charts we could get at Crosshaven in Cork. We started feeling more cheerful.

Having spent a pleasant day at Inishbofin, we sailed at 0800 on 11th July and motored south against a light head wind. The visibility was two miles and it began raining. The skipper had made a nonsense with the direction finder on Slyne Head; we stopped to sort things out and eventually sighted, at one mile, Slyne Head, a low, unfriendly headland; we rounded it at 1230, with no race to speak of. Visibility was improving as we motored eastwards, intending to go into Round-stone for the night. However, we got into a mess among the many rocks which were showing or breaking and which we could not identify; we were compelled, so to speak, to 'come out backwards'. We found that through mistaking Doon Hill for Mount Errisbeg (of which the top half was hidden in cloud), we had got well into Ballinaleama Bay. This mistake should have been obvious from the log reading,— which I had failed to note. A light breeze came from the west and we had a lovely, sunny afternoon's sail to Croagnakeela— or Deer—Island, with full mainsail for the first time this cruise. (To windward, *Yeong* is better with one panel down in the main.) We did not want to do the extra five miles up to Roundstone, so we then glided into Ard Bay (and as far up Little Ard Bay as seemed prudent at high water springs), to let go in three and a half fathoms at 1800. It was again a lovely evening and there was a good day's progress behind us, Slyne Head being our last headland before striking off for The Blaskets. Oh, for northerly winds. We enjoyed a good supper and cosy evening of chess.

The skipper was woken by nature at 0130 and was horrified to see, by the light of the moon behind a cloud, a large area of weed-covered rock, a foot above water only twenty feet away on our starboard side, and our keels by echo sounder still a foot off the bottom. A hasty

24

recourse to the tide tables showed that it should be just past low water and we calmed our nerves with cocoa while the tide rose, shuddering at the thought of what could have happened had we settled with one keel on the rock shelf.

The past three weeks on the coasts of Donegal, Mayo and Connemara had, in spite of bad weather and head winds, been a delightful experience and I would now like to go there again with time to explore The Rosses and thread the intricate channels leading between the many islets to such places as Rutland Harbour on the mainland opposite Aranmore, Blacksod Bay and, of course, the inlets of Roundstone, Kilkiran, Greatman, and Cashla in south Connemara. The scenery of blue-green mountains is magnificent, the foreground flecked with brilliant white flashes as the swell breaks on innumerable scattered rocks almost or completely awash. This coast was spendidly charted on large scale by the Navy a hundred years ago and one must pay attention to their warnings, for the swell is big and perpetual – even with no wind – and over a rocky patch with three or four fathoms. This swell can without warning break dangerously perhaps every five or ten minutes. To get an anchorage without swell, one has to go up the inlets, of which there are plenty. There are no steamers or large fishing vessels; almost no yachts; no officials; few inhabitants (and those all friendly), and no politics (although we did not meet many people).

On 12th July we weighed at 0545 and motored clear. A W Force 3/4 was forecast for Shannon. We hoped for a reach for the eighty miles to The Blaskets, motored as far as the Skird Rocks and there made sail at 0845, but the wind was south-westerly not westerly and we only just weathered Earagh Light on Inishmore (Aran Islands) at noon. It was overcast and cold. We sighted our first steamer during this cruise. Throughout the afternoon and evening we made disappointing tacks every two hours; our spirits were low. At 2200 the wind mercifully veered four points as the front passed and we were able to lay the course for The Blaskets.

The next day we sighted land ahead at 0600 and approached The Blaskets warily. We now had no chart of larger scale than 'Ireland West Coast', so we had to go outside; we had a worrying time identifying Inishtearacht as we could not see any lighthouse. We eventually discovered from our books that the lighthouse is on the other side of the islet. We rounded Inishtearacht at 1430, with an enormous swell breaking impressively on the various Blaskets. By an extensive study of the Admiralty Pilot we discovered the existence and whereabouts of The Fozes, rounded them, and anchored in Valentia at 2030. Here we began to see other yachts.

After two nights in Valentia, we sailed at 0920 on 15th July and beat slowly to the entrance in light airs from the north-west; we used the engine for forty minutes to help weather Reenard Point and for another hour from Puffin Island to Bolus Head, when the wind had fallen light. When aiming for Derrynane, for want of a larger scale chart, we had to go outside Scarriff Island, which we rounded at 1750. From there, a better breeze took us towards Derrynane. We enjoyed a glorious summer afternoon's sail with no swell. Approaching Derrynane in a freshening breeze we tried to lower the mainsail partly, to reduce speed, but it became foul just as we were in the narrowest part of the entrance and we had to make a dashing entry at 1910 under full sail; we let go among several yachts. Derrynane is a charming land-locked harbour, totally sheltered from swell and with a few scattered dwellings on the surrounding green hillside.

The 16th July was a lazy day of maintenance and washing clothes. There was a constant coming and going of French yachts who seem wisely to have taken over this delightful coast with its absence of officialdom – as Brittany was forty years ago. The next day was calm with the cloud base on the hillside down to two hundred feet. We motored out at 0805 bound for Crookhaven, or if the wind did not serve, Berehaven. Visibility was a half mile. We passed Maylaun Island at 0850 and shaped course for the Bull; after a while, we decided that with the ICC plan, Dursey Sound might be far easier for us than negotiating the herd of cattle in poor visibility and with no reasonable scale chart. We sighted Dursey Island at two miles and motored through the sound with a fair tide at 1115. We rounded Crow Head at 1200, stopped the engine and had a fine sail at four to six knots to Mizen Head, which we rounded at 1630. We then had a quiet run to Crookhaven, during which we were diverted three times by open fishing boats guarding miles of net. We finally beat in a Force 4/5 up to Crookhaven village to let go at 1830 under sail. It was a blustery evening, and we needed the Tilly lamp to keep warm while we had a quiet game of chess.

We had a fresh north-westerly wind on the 18th; we weighed at 1300 and had a fine run at seven knots under reduced sail to Schull, but had to beat up the bay to anchor off the pier at 1430 among some forty yachts, again largely French. We persuaded an old man to let us have fourteen gallons of diesel fuel.

During the winter of 1940 I had been sent in a destroyer to observe Long Island Sound at night after a rumour of a U-boat in the area. I had seen nothing. I told this to the old man who sold us the diesel fuel and was interested when he said: 'Oh, yes. They used to come in for supplies.'

On 19th July we weighed at 0915 and, with the wind W Force 3, sailed over to have a look at the tiny north harbour on Cape Clear Island. We turned round in the entrance and had a memorable sail to Baltimore by the north entrance. Once we had identified Hare Island (our best chart being 'Valentia to Cork'), the excellent plan in the ICC book was quite adequate. The anchorage off the village was too rough for our dinghy, so we let go at 1205 above the RNLI slip and went ashore there for provisions.

The 20th July was dull and cold with a SW Force 2/3. We weighed at 0930, motored to the entrance and had a nice run to Castletownshend, where we entered in a squall and let go close into the landing place at 1200. We had no outboard and were glad to get this berth before the crowd arrived for Monday's party. We had achieved the object of our cruise with a couple of days in hand for cleaning up, so we celebrated with a smashing dinner *chez* Mary Ann, our only meal ashqre throughout this cruise. We exchanged one or two visits, notably with Paul Dane, who most kindly lent us a couple of charts to take us as far as Dublin. Yachts streamed in throughout the next two days until there were 160 at anchor.

The ICC organized the whole jubilee celebration and cruise-in-company superbly and the next day, after the party ashore on 23rd July, we watched the yachts leaving westwards and then rather sadly started *our* course eastwards, spending that night in Glandore. We had the benefit of fair winds and spent nights in Kinsale, Crosshaven, Ballycotton, Helvick, and Dunmore East, where we spent three uncomfortable days in a gale. There were seven larger boats outside us and our fenders were near bursting and were squealing loudly until lubricated with washing-up liquid. A neighbour gave us directions for Wexford, which is said to be silted up and closed, with all marks withdrawn. After a night in Rosslare, we ventured towards Wexford. The bar and the six-mile channel that winds across an open piece of water the size of Chichester Harbour are marked by unofficial buoys laid by the local sailing club. The cans are of all shapes and sizes and are sometimes a mile apart and very difficult to find; but it was fun and worth-while. Wexford is an important county town with good shops. Thanks to the Chinese characters for 'kingfisher' on our wind vane we got rid of talkative small boys by saying, 'Only speakee Chinese.'

We left Wexford at 0915, 4th August. We took three hours to get to the bar after we mistook a buoy and grounded gently several times while getting out of the narrow channel. We then had a grand sail at six knots and over inside the banks to Wicklow. It was as well that we had the 'Small Craft Notices to Mariners' as many of the buoys had been changed the previous spring. The quays up the river are now excellent for yachts and are being further improved. There we lay for three nights with gale conditions outside.

On 7th August the wind fell to NW Force 3 in the afternoon and we sailed at 1515, when we were just able to lay the course up the coast. Later the wind failed, then went dead ahead Force 5, so we motor-beat. We had intended getting to Howth but it was rain squalls and murk off the Muglins and we decided to make for Kingstown (now called something unpronounceable by the natives) and anchored at 2030.

The following day we had a pleasant fast reach past Malahide and Rogerstown to anchor in Lough Shinny. This cove makes a splendid anchorage in which to wait for the tide across the forty-mile bay to St. John's Point, where the Irish Sea tides split, enabling one to carry a fair tide for twelve hours. During the night, the barometer dropped sharply as a front came through; the wind whistled in the rigging, the chain ground over rock and we spent an uneasy night dozing in our oilskin trousers. The wind did not drop and begin to back until midday. At 1530 we weighed and shaped course for St. John's Point, close hauled on the port tack. After Rockabill it fell light and we motored all afternoon and evening, bound for Ardglass where we wanted to clear customs. It was 0310 on 10th August by the time we passed St. John's Point and began looking for Ardglass. We saw shore lights and approached them with confidence but when we got within half a mile, we still could not identify the leading light and from what we could see of the dark shore of the bay, it did not seem to be the right shape. We concluded that Ardglass must be round the next point. (We later found that this must have been Killough, not shown at all on the only chart we had. We must have been blundering about among a lot of drying rocks in its approach. God was *very* kind to us on this cruise.) Rounding the next point we opened up the lights of what must surely be Ardglass, but we could not see the sectored light. We stopped and waited for daylight so we could see the entrance. The lighthouse was there right enough but it could not have been work-ing. We anchored off the fish pier at 0630, feeling rather weary. There are no longer customs at Ardglass and after a short sleep we weighed at 1115 on 10th August and, all afternoon, had a good sail to the Galloway coast. It was heavily overcast and could enough for me to wear an ex-army great coat over everything else. At 1900, when we were two miles short of Port Patrick, the spring tide turned against us and it called for seven knots with engine, plus a fair breeze, to get us into that tiny cavernous pocket at 2015.

We took the fair tide at 1320 the next day and with a fair wind, sailed in blazing sun towards Arran. As we approached Holy Island, however, there was thick drizzle and as darkness fell we had difficulty seeing the lights at the south entrance to Lamlash. We were not helped by the fact that the Holy Isle south light had been changed from red to green and the Fullerton Rock buoy from white to red. We anchored off King's Cross at 2230.

The morning of 12th August was drizzly but it cleared up a bit. We weighed at 1150 and had a lovely sail past Brodick and up to Sannox, after which there were squalls and heavy rain all the way to Tarbert, where we found our mooring free at 1755.

TABLE OF DISTANCES

	Distance made good	Time h.m.	Knots	Engine time h.m.
Tarbert – L. Ranza	11	2.45	4.0	0.30
L. Ranza – Lamlash	27	5.15	5.1	1.30
Lamlash – Campbeltown	26	12.35	2.1	4.05
Campbeltown – Sanda Island	12	5.00	2.4	3.45
Sanda Island – Portrush	40	8.45	4.5	4.05
Portrush – Inishtrahull	26	6.00	4.3	5.15
Inishtrahull – Port Salon	20	4.15	4.7	4.15
Port Salon – Sheephaven	20	6.15	3.0	3.15
Sheephaven – Kincashla	27	8.15	3.2	8.15
Kincashla – Aran Road	8	2.15	3.5	1.45
Aran Road – Teelin	35	7.30	4.6	2.30
Teelin – Killibegs	10	2.35	4.3	0.00
Killibegs – Teelin	10	3.20	3.1	3.20
Teelin – Broadhaven	56	12.50	4.4	11.40
Broadhaven – Blacksod Quay	29	11.35	2.5	3.45
Blacksod Quay – Inishbofin	36	11.40	3.1	2.45
Inishbofin – Ard Bay	28	10.00	2.8	5.55
Ard Bay – Valentia	78	38.45	2.5	5.25
Valentia – Derrynane	24	9.50	2.5	1.40
Derrynane – Crookhaven	33	10.15	3.2	3.55
Crookhaven – Schull	9	1.30	6.0	0.00
Schull – Baltimore	11	2.50	3.5	0.00
Baltimore – Castletownshend	12	2.30	4.8	0.25
Castletownshend – Glandore	7	2.00	3.5	0.25
Glandore – Kinsale	31	8.45	3.5	3.50
Kinsale – Crosshaven	17	5.30	3.1	3.50
Crosshaven – Ballycotton	17	3.45	4.5	0.10
Ballycotton – Helvick	25	5.15	4.7	0.00
Helvick – Dunmore East	24	4.10	5.8	0.00
Dunmore East – Rosslare	37	8.30	4.3	2.10
Rosslare – Wexford	11	2.55	3.8	2.55
Wexford – Wicklow	48	8.10	5.2	0.30
Wicklow – Kingstown	22	5.15	4.2	3.10
Kingstown – L. Shinny	16	4.40	3.4	0.00
L. Shinny – Ardglass	48	12.00	4.0	11.15
Ardglass – Port Patrick	41	8.30	5.0	0.30
Port Patrick – Lamlash	42	9.00	4.7	3.50
Lamlash – Tarbert	27	6.05	4.4	0.00
Total Trip	1,021	292	(3.5)	109

Fuel used: 36 gallons

EIGHTY YEARS OF SAILING

by E.J.C. Edwards

Over the past eighty years I have been fortunate enough to sail in a variety of craft in various parts of the world. As some of these craft are no longer in existence I am venturing to write down a few of my reminiscences for those who share my love of the sea and a jolly sail.

My sailing experience started at the turn of the century on the Canoe Lake, Ryde, on the Isle of Wight. There is often a healthy breeze on the front and as a small boy of nine I enjoyed myself speeding round the basin in a beautifully varnished little boat about 7ft. long. Meanwhile the owner, a dumpy chap, stood on the bank and shouted instructions to me. I could not afford the three-pence hire fee very often, so I used to clean the boats for him in return for a sail.

It was always my ambition to become a Naval Officer, but astigmatism prevented me entering the Service. Instead, after a glorious summer messing about in a sailing dinghy in Sandown Bay, away from my school books, I joined HMS *Worcester*, Thames Nautical Training College in 1905. *Worcester* had been a full-rigged ship of the line during the days when the Navy was under sail.

During one of my holidays I made my first cruise with my young brother Harold. We hired a sailing punt at Caversham and had a happy week's cruise up to Oxford and back. It was a fine sailing boat, flat-bottomed with leeboards, about 20ft. long and with a 4ft. beam. We slept on board the punt under the sail, a big standing lug, and when it rained we tried to find shelter under a bridge. My mother gave us four shillings pocket-money and some food, including a tasty ham. It was lucky I could fish: a dog ran off with our ham early on in the cruise.

In the *Worcester* I served a period as captain's coxswain. My charge was the captain's gig (less people went in lesser boats), a beautifully kept four-oared boat in which I rowed the captain and his wife the quarter-mile stretch from the ship to the causeway at Greenhithe.

The top form was taught navigation by 'Old Noodle', a famous navigation teacher. Whenever we were being more than usually dense, he would point to the muck-barges carrying the soil of London out to sea and exclaim that we would be lucky if we managed to rise to the command of one of these.

On leaving the *Worcester* in 1908 I was top of the ship. I collected several prizes (including a sextant) and was one of the boys accepted as RNR probationary midshipman. I did my first RNR drill on HMS *Mars*, an old ship with two funnels side by side, and gained much kudos by winning the cutter race in the fleet sports.

I was then apprenticed to Geo. Milne & Co of Aberdeen and served my time in the *Inverurie*, a barque of 1,309 tons register and 242ft. LOA. I made three voyages to Australia in her; two of them with general cargo – first to Fremantle in eighty-nine days returning via the Cape of Good Hope, then to Sydney in 114 days. My third voyage was to Montevideo with a cargo of coal and thence in ballast to Adelaide. I returned from my voyages to Sydney and Adelaide via Cape Horn; from Sydney in 124 days, from Adelaide in 120. As an apprentice my pay was five shillings a week in port, nothing at sea. I once went eight months without going ashore.

In the *Worcester* we had been trained to go aloft and lay out on the yard. My first night at sea on 24th October 1908, after the *Inverurie* had been towed out of Garston Docks, Liverpool, I was sent aloft to loose the main royals. It was the custom in this ship that the boys generally dealt with the royals and the men the headsails. It was blowing hard and I was scared stiff and sick all the way up and down the rigging. In fact I was sick throughout most of my first three weeks at sea – but never again. Going aloft has never bothered me since; it's only during the last two or three years, since I reached the age of eighty-five, that I have not been aloft to do necessary repairs in my own little ship. However, I never had the head for heights of one dare-devil in the *Inverurie* who, when we were in Fremantle alongside the quay with the yards squared, would run along the bare foreyard and dive off the end.

The worst job aloft was greasing the masts in the sections where the hoisting yards moved. Every Saturday morning, almost regardless of weather, a boy was sent aloft with a can of slush from the galley. You had to slide down, gripping the mast with your knees and one hand, and dab the slush on with the other.

I fell from aloft on my first voyage, although not while doing that job. I was working aloft with another boy, setting up a purchase on a lashing on the jaws of the gaff; we did something silly and fell. I fell across the ship's rail, half in and half out of the ship; the other boy landed on top of me. I broke his fall, so he was all right; but after a while I found that I couldn't pee. I was in agony and went to the Old Man. I was laid out on the after hatch and given a slug of rum as an anaesthetic. The Old Man's ally in all medical work was Chips (the carpenter), who would read the book of instructions to the Old Man as the operation proceeded. During my operation there was a long pause. Then I heard the Old Man say, 'Chips! Chips! You bloody fool. You've turned over two pages at once.' I went to the Old Man afterwards and asked him what he had done. 'Put you right, haven't I, boy? Get back to work.' To this day I do not know what he did.

It was wonderful to see the way the Old Man (J.W. Holmes) handled the *Inverurie*. When we were loading wheat in the Spencer Gulf and picking up the grain from long jetties, we would drop anchor and back into the jetty as if *Inverurie* had an engine and was going to lie stern-to in a Mediterranean harbour. But we had no engine, of course, and weighing was a day's job: one turn of the capstan was about one link of chain.

We were approaching Queenstown for orders when a tug came out and bartered with the Old Man for a tow in. 'You'd better take a tow in, mister,' called the tugboat skipper, 'the wind's going to change.' 'Be told by a tug skipper what the wind's going to do? Never!' cried the Old Man, 'Take your filthy smoke-stack away.' The wind did change and we had to beat our way into Queenstown. This was quite a job for a ship that size with a deck crew of six apprentices and eight men, but it was very thrilling, and the captain must have had complete confidence in his ship and his crew to do it.

It was exciting to be at the wheel of the *Inverurie* with a spread of canvas high above you. The seventy-year-old mate was a former captain who, under him, had had seven ships sold to foreigners. He made me realise how little money there was in the Mercantile Marine. When I got my ticket of second mate I was offered a job by Geo. Milne at £6 10s per month, I turned it down.

I went for another RNR drill on HMS *Zealandia*, during which I often saw newspaper advertisements for interesting jobs. I got a day's leave and went up to London with a list of eleven jobs to make enquiries. The first few were no good, but then I came to the office of a rubber-planting company. The secretary of the firm asked me what I wanted. I explained I had come in response to their advertisement. 'You're in luck,' he said, 'There's a board meeting on.' I was taken into the board room and met three old gentlemen. 'What do you know about rubber?' one of them asked. 'I think it grows on a bush,' I replied. There were roars of laughter from the board. 'What do you have to recommend yourself?' 'I've got a second mate's ticket in sail in my pocket,' I replied. 'You must be tough,' said the chairman. 'We'll take you.'

In 1912 I went out to Malaya as junior assistant on a rubber plantation in the state of Perak on the – to me – princely wage of £17 per month, even more than my captain was earning.

On the estate, Sengat, there was a fourteen-acre lake surrounded by rubber trees and as soon as I could afford it, I had a little boat built. I found my riches did not go as far as I had expected; even I, in my humble position, had to employ a cook, a boy and a *tukan-ayer* (water-carrier). The Chinese cook would draw a week's money in advance on Monday and head straight for Ipoh, nine miles away, to gamble. If he did well I lived like a lord; if he did badly I had a thin week.

The estate carpenter had never seen a boat in his life but, working from the pictures I showed him, built my boat. It was a simple flat-bottomed boat with a dagger-board. He was convinced that the water would come up the dagger-board trunking and sink the boat. (He was astounded when it floated.) The boat was fastened with iron nails; the rig was a large standing lug, cut out on the floor of my bungalow by the local tailor.

I once had a very happy cruise down the Perak river, starting from Parit and passing through out-of-the-way places which were little known in those days and for which the river was the only form of transport. My crew comprised my manager and a friend of his. At night we stayed in little Malay houses. The voyage finished at Teluk Anson, where the boat was carried to Sengat on a bullock-cart.

There were frequent bathing parties at the falls of Menlinshaw, at the top of which was a wide, stony, moss-covered ledge. With the help of a good push from a friend, we would sit on banana leaves and ride over the waterchute. You splashed down in a deep pool at the bottom – usually without your banana leaf.

At the outbreak of the First World War, I joined up in Singapore and was sent to Mesopotamia. I was appointed No. 1 in PS95, one of the largest paddlers working up and down the Tigris. The campaign was dependent on the Tigris for the transportation of both men and supplies, and the battles of that unknown war were fought within reach of the river. The temperature in summer went up to 120°; at night, when it came down to 90°, we thought it was cool. In winter there was sometimes a film of ice on the water in the fire buckets.

The ships were paddle steamers, most of them from Indian rivers. They drew no more than five feet of water and always towed one barge on either side of the ship; the biggest paddlers could carry a thousand troops distributed between ship and barges. We carried troops and supplies to the front and wounded soldiers from it.

In PS95 I served under a tough skipper, Shepherd, who was prepared to let go in any weather – even a sand-storm – and would keep going any night. This wanted a lot of nerve. The navigable channel had a sand bottom, without rocks, and was always shifting and although marked by stakes, was unlit. Under Shepherd's leadership I had plenty of experience in getting the ship off after we had gone aground. He was a great bridge-player and after we had had a grounding would say, 'Number One! Let me know when she's off.' Then he would go below and play bridge with the officer-passengers. While he became increasingly proficient at bridge, I became more and more efficient at getting a stranded vessel afloat.

The barges were made fast with fibre rope so that if the ship came up all-standing, the rope, not the bitts, broke. To get the ship afloat the drill was to send the boat off and drive long stakes into the desert and use these to kedge off. When the stakes came home the boat was sent to drive in more; the leadsmen were constantly sounding and their cries got on everyone's nerves. Seven feet was no bottom.

When Shepherd went sick in April 1918, I took over command of PS95 with the rank of lieutenant in the Inland Water Transport, Royal Engineers. I brought the ship into Kut to berth alongside for the very first time. After all engines had been shut off, the engineer came to see me. 'I'm leaving this ship,' he said. 'Why, Kroll?' 'To berth this ship Captain Shepherd used to give three engine orders: forward, astern, off engines. Do you know how many orders you gave? Nineteen! I've had it.' However, he did not leave the ship and I soon learned how to berth it.

Shortly after I took over, we were carrying some Indian troops when there was a dreadful outbreak of bubonic plague. The ship was sent to a backwater where I had the carpenters make a dinghy for me. I had some jolly sailing in it and hoped to bring it back to the UK with me; unfortunately it was stolen.

I was appalled by the callous attitude to life in India. To tighten up a nut on one of the paddles, an Indian fitter climbed on to the wheel with an enormous spanner made fast to his belt. The poor fellow lost his grip, fell into the speeding river and weighed down by the spanner, was lost to view. 'Damn!' said his overseer. 'We haven't got another spanner that size.'

When the Tigris was at the flood the current was fearsome. The ship made full speed whether we were going with the current or against it, either to stem the current or to keep control when coming down with it. If we were anchored and had orders to go downstream it was a problem to turn round. At least we had an enormous 16ft. rudder; I developed the art of backing away gently until the rudder just touched and then letting the current bring the ship round.

Not only did we carry men, but also animals — often horses, occasionally camels. We were once bringing up a load of mules when one of the animals broke loose, jumped over the side, swam ashore and trotted along the river-bank in company with us. The subaltern in charge, the son of the colonel of the regiment, asked if I would stop to pick the mule up. He had brought the mules all the way from North India without having lost one; now, with Dad almost literally round the next bend, he was anxious to complete his charge with a full complement of animals. I agreed that he could try to capture the runaway.

While we were banking in, he and some fellow officers swam their horses ashore and tried to round up the mule. The men would almost have him cornered but he would give them the slip and they would have to start again. The animal was having a wonderful game. As we had arranged, I allowed them twenty minutes and then gave a warning hoot. The young men worked even harder. At thirty minutes I gave a second hoot. They reluctantly turned their horses away from the mule and trotted on board. Suddenly, when we were just about to raise the gangway, the mule galloped across the desert, raced up the gangway and went straight to his place in the stalls.

Some of the big paddlers were brought home to England after the war with a view to being sent to Russia. I came as navigator in one PA1 in the spring of 1919. It was a worrying voyage as the paddlers had very little freeboard and we were always concerned about running out of fuel. I was finally demobbed in Southampton.

Loudon Shand, my employers before the war, had been most kind in granting me a small allowance while I was serving. When I was demobbed I received a telegram from the chairman of the company saying, 'War is over. Your allowance is over. Get back to the job.' I had been assistant on Sengat and expected to go back there, but they gave me the management of Teluk Piah, a 700-acre rubber estate on the Selangor coast.

I went to the Transport Officer at Winchester to be repatriated to Malaya. 'Ah yes,' he said, 'that's via Vancouver and Shanghai.' '*You're* the Transport Officer,' I replied. So my wife and I had a wonderful honeymoon journey by train across Canada, by ship to Shanghai and then on to Singapore. Off the China coast the ship ran into a dreadful storm, a real typhoon, which was most unpleasant.

My estate of Teluk Piah was fronted on one side by the Selangor river and on another by the sea. I had three yachts built for me by Malay builders while I was there: *Imp*, a day-boat; *Mawnan*, a five-tonner; and *Mat Ali*, eleven tons.

There was an 18ft. rise and fall to the river. I had a catwalk built for high tide, but when the river was low I would get into my dinghy, get a shove down the slope and toboggan down the mud into the water. This was fun – especially when I tobogganed down the slope, splashed into the water and collided with a crocodile who had been snoozing just on the surface. He was a wicked great fellow, but fortunately he was as alarmed as I was and made off.

There was a government bounty of fifty cents a foot for catching crocodiles. The Malays had a wonderful way of catching the crocs in the river. All that was wanted was a little bit of bamboo (cut from the jungle) about a foot long and pointed at both ends, about twenty feet of copper wire (usually telegraph wire), a four-gallon kerosene tin and a hen (probably stolen). The hen was soaked in poison and speared with the bamboo, which had the tin tied to it by the copper wire. All this was taken to the river. The croc would see the nice fat hen and swallow it; the poison then took two or three days to work. The kerosene tin acted as a marker: as the croc moved he dragged it with him. All the Malay fisherman had to do was wait until the tin was still; then he knew the croc was dead and he could haul him up and collect his reward.

On one occasion I had to visit an estate on the east coast of Malaya to make a valuation. There was no road up the coast then, but it was arranged that I should pick up the estate launch at Kuantan. I arrived at the appointed time but found that the launch was not ready to leave. I did not want to wait; so made enquiries and hired a local boat, about forty feet long with a lateen sail and a small motor. It was a lovely day's sail; we left before breakfast and got in by evening. I made my valuation and we started the return trip. Soon after getting away a heavy squall blew up. I wanted to stand out to sea but the crew did not and stood in for the shore. A small, ramshackle fishing village stood at a little river-mouth — more of a cove but offering practically no shelter. At the entrance to the river-mouth there was quite a bar; we hit it heavily and the boat capsized. We struggled ashore but I had lost my papers and money. The local coffee shop was run by a Chinese man who, without knowing anything about me and with no security, gave me some clothes and lent me enough money to get back home.

In 1934 my yacht *Mat Ali* was built without any power tools under a shade of attap. She was gaff-rigged and built to the Harrison Butler 'Khamseen' design. I named her after her builder, whose father had been hanged by the British as a pirate. 'Dad made one mistake,' said old Mat, 'he was caught.' I had several years' sailing in Malaya with her. Sailing in Malaya is dominated by the off-shore breezes by night and the on-shore breeze by day. My hand, an ex-fisherman, and I often fished together.

In 1937 I had *Mat Ali* shipped to Port Said and from there sailed her to England. I intended to go via the Bay of Biscay but this was the time of the Spanish Civil War and I was advised to go via the Midi Canal. As it was, I was in great trouble at Ustica. We had had a long slow passage, water was getting low and so I decided to put in at Ustica, which was then, although I did not know it, an Italian prison island. As soon as I stepped ashore I was arrested. The prison authorities had learnt that an escape was to be made with the aid of a visiting yacht. I was kept ashore for three days, not in prison but in a hotel — which I had to pay for — while they checked my credentials and confirmed our route from Port Said. My two companions were worse off. On board they had the permanent company of a large policeman who snored badly. We were finally allowed to sail when our innocence was proven, although I was supposed to sail to a major Italian port and make my number with the authorities there. Needless to say, as soon as we were out of sight we headed straight for French soil.

The problem with taking *Mat Ali* through the French canals was that she drew nearly six feet. I assured the authorities that by the time the mast, anchors and heavy gear were out (I had them sent ahead on a barge), we should be well down. However, we bumped on nearly every cill! Our worst grounding was at Toulon, right outside the company's head office. Quick as a flash my French crew,

Emil, rushed into the office to complain of the lack of water. They admitted sadly that they were rather behind with their dredging.

We sailed into the Helford River one summer afternoon. I saw a woman and boy sitting on the beach having tea and called to my crew, 'There's my son and wife!' Instantly, Jim dived overboard, fully clothed, swam ashore and introduced himself.

I was invited to go drift-net fishing with some Cornish fishermen. We drifted with the tide, and at lunch-time I produced my little packet of sandwiches. 'You don't want that. Have some real grub,' they said and produced a bit of fat pork. I choked it down, then started to pour some tea from my vacuum flask. 'You don't want that. Have a real brew,' they said and produced some dreadful stuff that had been stewing on the hob and was stiff with sugar. I got that down and started to fill my pipe. 'You don't want that. Have some real baccy,' they said and produced some plug. It was awful; I couldn't manage it at all and ran for the lee rail. They were much amused. 'Come and see the yachtsman,' they cried. The crew lined the rail to watch me being sick.

We were out of sight of land and as we turned for home, I asked the skipper how he knew where to go. 'Been here before,' he said. 'But how do you know what course to steer?' I asked. 'Where's the compass?' 'We've got a compass,' he replied; 'of course we have. Couldn't get our BoT certificate without it.' He turned to his mate and said, 'Where's the compass.' The mate ferreted around and produced an old cracked compass which was quite useless to anyone. Without taking the slightest interest in it the skipper steered us from nowhere straight back to Porthleven.

I sailed *Mat Ali* around Great Britain during the summer of 1938, taking her through the Pentland Firth. There was no wind and at the crucial moment the petrol-paraffin engine petered out and we started to drift with the powerful tide. A phrase from the *Pilot* came to mind: 'A sailing vessel without way is doomed to destruction.' We came close to the rocks but a breeze sprang up in the nick of time and we escaped.

In the last Fastnet before the Second World War, I was mate of a watch in Pip Holman's cutter *Morva*. Having rounded the Fastnet we came roaring back with a glorious fair wind under spinnaker. Then the spinnaker blew out. 'Set the other!' commanded Pip. We were just overtaking a little coaster; the skipper of this small craft went into his bridge-house and came out on to the bridge wearing a bowler hat, which he solemnly doffed to us. I spent the first night of the war alone in *Mat Ali* at sea. I was taking her down to the West Country and at Torquay my crew, Margaret Leonard, received a telegram recalling her. The authorities had been ordered to clear the harbour. I had dinner ashore and then pushed off in *Mat Ali*. However, I found there were no navigation lights and I had to round Start Point. Despite this drawback it was a pleasant sail with a light head wind and on a fine night.

I arrived at Port Navas to find my wife in a state of excitement. A telegram had arrived for me which said, 'On presentation of this telegram at any railway station you will be given a ticket to London.' I hardly did a thing to lay up *Mat Ali* and caught the night train to London. I had volunteered for the Thames Patrol and had command of the Erith to Ford Motor Works section of the river. I arranged exercises for the patrol boats which were launches and motorboats manned by their owners, all plain-clothes volunteers, and we established a form of communication manned by Sea Cadets.

After exercises we met in a pub at Erith to discuss the work. One of the skippers always had his launch back before anyone else and took the best seat by the fire. I was determined to beat this habit. Five minutes before an exercise was due to end the Sea Cadet on board his launch passed my signal to him: 'Your stoker has fallen down the companionway and must be taken to hospital forthwith.' The nearest hospital was some distance and I was staggered on entering the pub to find him, as usual, in the best seat by the fire. I sent for the signal book and read his reply, 'Regret stoker has died of his injuries. Am landing the body at the causeway.' I stood him a beer.

After a couple of months in the Thames Patrol I decided to go on active service. I went for an interview at an office in St. James'. The interviewer, a captain RN, asked my age. 'As I'm not yet in uniform, sir,' I said, 'can I ask you some questions? What's the oldest you send a man to sea?' 'About forty,' he replied. 'How fortunate; I still have two years to go,' I said, thus knocking ten years off my age. The captain merely replied, 'If you pass the medical I am prepared to accept that statement.'

I volunteered for mine-sweeping and was posted to Sheerness with the rank of lieutenant RNVR. In due course I was given my own command, a beautifully converted steel trawler which — I was delighted to find — was named HMS *Edwardian* and was fitted with Oropesa sweeps for clearing moored mines. I had a grand crew, all ex-trawlermen. Once, we had a mine adrift and it floated half-submerged in the water. The crew fired away at it with rifles but still the mine bobbed about. What usually happened was that the mine would crack when it was about to sink; occasionally a shot would hit one of the horns and the mine would explode. While the crew fired, I said I would steam round to the other side to get a better light on the mine. I was round-it rather close when somebody shouted, 'Let Slushy have a go.' Slushy was the cook and a hopeless shot, so hopeless I had stopped sending him to rifle practice with the rest of the crew — it was a waste of ammunition. Slushy picked up the rifle, shut his eyes tight and pressed the trigger. The mine did not sink — it blew up. It was much too close to us and our electrics and crockery suffered. On our way back we passed through a bit of an air raid, so I found it easy to write off our damage.

During the Dunkirk evacuation of June 1940 *Edwardian* was involved in keeping the channels free from mines and in assisting any launch in trouble. It was really wonderful how totally unsuitable craft, commanded by grand chaps who had probably never used a chart in their lives before, were making the crossing.

No women were allowed in the volunteer crews. One day *Edwardian* was in for fuel and I went over to *Wildfire* (our HQ) for a drink in the bar. An owner came up to the captain of *Wildfire* with whom I was talking. He explained that he was trying to get an engine part, which he had seen in the store, but had been told he was not entitled to have it. The captain grabbed the phone, had a sharp conversation, handed the receiver to the owner and said, 'Now tell him what you want and tell him to bring it here. Meanwhile, have a drink.' 'No thank you, sir,' the owner said looking awkward; 'I won't hang about here. My crew's waiting outside.' 'Bring him in!' replied the captain. 'Well,' said the owner, even more awkwardly, 'my crew is my wife.' 'But you know women are not allowed,' exclaimed the captain. 'I know,' the owner replied; 'but my wife has made the crossing twice already and I can't handle the ship without her.' The captain turned to me and said, 'Get back to your ship,' and took the man and his crew off to his cabin.

On 11th August 1940, *Edwardian* and another trawler were carrying out a sweep off Ramsgate. A violent air battle was in progress and I was signalled to take my partner towards North Foreland to pick up survivors. Suddenly, out of the hubbub overhead, a German dive-bomber swooped over us, flying very low. I was on the bridge watching the firing when there was a loud explosion in *Edwardian*. A bomb had been dropped on us. Our gunner blazed away and our enemy burst into flames and careered into the sea.

I gave the order to head *Edwardian* in-shore with the intention of beaching her. We were about two miles off-shore, but I don't think we moved. The engine-room was a shambles and the engine-room staff were lost. *Edwardian* just sank. We swam and held on to floating wreckage; we helped those who could not swim (including Slushy). It was a warm sunny afternoon and there was not much of a sea. My sister ship, under Catchpole, had also been heavily plastered with bombs but did a wonderful job picking up those of us who survived and we struggled back to Sheerness in her, everyone pumping like mad. *Edwardian* was later raised.

After serving as a Unit Officer at Sheerness for some months I was appointed to the staff at Singapore as Mine-sweeping Officer with the rank of lieutenant-commander. They had asked for someone who had had practical experience of mine-sweeping to come and help their keen but inexperienced chaps. My work there also included visits to Hong Kong and Rangoon.

I had left *Mat Ali* in a mud berth at Port Navas and before I went abroad I went to see how she was. She was in a terrible state. Somebody had been on board, used the loo and left the sea-cock open. Water and mud were all over the cabin. I sold her — almost gave her away — quickly, just as she was, I have not seen *Mat Ali* since, but I have been in correspondence with a recent owner.

Before leaving England I was called to Buckingham Palace to be decorated. The sweepers based on Sheerness, of which *Edwardian* had been one, had maintained a steady and perpetual routine in the approaches to the Thames. I had had a pretty lively time sweeping and was fortunate still to be alive; but alive I was and with two DSCs to my credit. One of the nicest things of the day I went to Buckingham Palace was the taxi driver who drove me there. He refused to take my fare, saying it was an honour to have me aboard his cab. In the Palace ante-room some dignified gentlemen in long black coats were telling us what the form was when I met Kent, a fellow, who had been a new boy with me on the *Worcester*. I am afraid we yarned away instead of giving full attention to the little lecture.

My name was finally called. In I went and King George spoke to me; 'I see you have two DSCs; why didn't you come before?' 'Couldn't get any leave, sir.' His Majesty laughed, 'Always the same in the Navy.'

I was sent out to Singapore in the spring of 1941 by sea. When my duties in Singapore allowed, I went sailing at the Royal Singapore Yacht Club of which I had long been a member. I was most fortunate in buying a six-metre yacht in partnership with Commander Geoff Packard RN, another member of staff. The yacht had broken its mast and the previous owner was in despair over getting it mended; but I had happened to meet a shipwright from Mashford's yard in the naval dockyard and he was able to rebuild the mast for me. The week after buying the yacht, 'Pack' and I were racing it.

The two months of war following the Japanese invasion of Malaya on 7th December 1941 soon brought Singapore to a wretched state; there were bodies, rubble, refuse, smoke, and stench everywhere. I knew — everyone knew — that the next day we would be in the bag. I jumped up. 'Why?' I said to myself. I had no responsibility for any staff, 'Why not try to get away?' But I thought I should get permission to go, otherwise I might be accused of deserting. So I went to the chief-of-staff, Captain 'Hooky' Bell and asked to speak to the Admiral. 'Hooky' asked my business and I explained that I wanted to make a getaway in my six-metre. 'You're mad,' said 'Hooky', 'but I'll speak to the Admiral on one condition.' 'What's that?' I asked. 'That I come too.' 'Well, sir,' I said, 'I have nothing against you personally but you're a captain and I'm a lieutenant-commander and I expect that like many naval officers you don't know much about sailing small boats.' 'You're right,' laughed 'Hooky', 'I'll sign on as A/B Bell.'

'Delighted to have you then, sir,' I said. 'Pack' of course came too and we collected a staff doctor. In the street I met a broker friend, Ned Holliday, dressed in the uniform of the local regiment, and I invited him to come as well. 'I'd love too,' he said sadly, 'but I've my men to think of.' We wished each other luck and parted.

Tinned food for our passage was easy to come by, although we had no tin-opener. Water, however, was a great problem. We obtained some four-gallon tins and filled them, but we could not seal them. There was scarcely a soul in the streets, but one of the few remaining servants in the Club took the tins away and found a tinsmith who soldered on a seal.

Down at the jetty our hopes fell: my six-metre was waterlogged. A shell had fallen nearby and blown a hole in the side. However, still afloat on its mooring was a six-metre belonging to an RAF member who I knew had already left the country. The Club boatmen and the boat had vanished. We swam out to the six-metre, brought it in as near to the jetty as possible, then waded out with our gear and loaded it on the yacht. I suddenly remembered we had no tin-opener, ran up to the Club House to get one and also some cutlery and china. I took the things and the boy presented me with the chit to sign. As I signed, exploding shells shook the ground nearby. I ran down to the yacht and loaded up. At last we got the sails on board and got away. We brought out my mainsail from my locker, struggled out with it to the yacht and hove it on board. It was no use. My mainsail was for a track, the airman's needed hanks. We splashed ashore again. His locker was secured by the biggest padlock I have ever seen and all we could find to smash it was a stone. Finally, something gave way and we found his sail.

By now it was well into the night. We made sail and slipped away on the light breeze. Suddenly, gunshots fell near us. 'They've got our range,' Pack said, 'the next one will get us. I as a gunnery officer tell you!' He kept repeating this until we eventually told him to shut up. Dawn was coming, and the tide turned against us. We drifted back into the main harbour and picked up a buoy. The guns were silent; this was the moment of defeat. We pulled the cover over the cockpit and lay on the floor. It was stifling. I took a wary look around at some time during the day and saw our warp was not too well secured; with great care I poked a hand out to take another turn. When darkness fell we let go again, floated out on the tide, and then set sail. My plan was to go north about of Sumatra, put in for water and supplies at a small port on the northern tip and then ride the monsoon to Ceylon. We had a compass and a chart of the Indian Ocean; I reckoned we should be there in a week to ten days – or not at all.

The day wore on. There was a fair wind and we were doing well. Then on the horizon, a ship appeared, possibly a Japanese vessel. The others lay flat on the floor, their revolvers at the ready. I sat in the cockpit wearing only a sarong and my deep sun tan. The ship closed us; she was full of Japanese soldiers. I waved to them cheerily, shouted out a Malay greeting, and the ship steamed on.

We pressed our yacht hard but, during the night, the port chain-plate dragged out. 'Pack' was a first-class sailor and instantly swung the yacht on to the starboard tack, thus saving the mast; but it was obvious that sailing to Ceylon was out of the question. We closed the coast of Sumatra and in daylight entered a river-mouth, where there was a village which I had once visited in *Mat Ali*. We had made good about a hundred miles up the Sumatra coast. There was a hospital in the village and we asked the nurses if they would like to join our party. We were planning to head over the mountains for Padang on the west coast. The nurses declined, saying they should stay with their patients. We presented them with the yacht and set off for Padang, getting a lift whenever we could, although very few people had petrol and we had little money to pay for it.

There was a number of wireless stations in Sumatra and 'Hooky' knew that HMS *Danae*, under a Commander Butler, was off the west coast looking for survivors and refugees. He put out a message, which I think was, 'The bell is ringing for the butler.' The reply came: 'The butler will be calling at midnight.'

When we arrived in Padang we found a crowd of refugees, who had crossed the straits, and several survivors of sunken ships. We thought our troubles were over when we stepped aboard *Danae*, but Commander Butler received orders to get rid of all the passengers who he had rescued. He landed the ninety or so of us in Tjilitjap in Java. By this time the Japanese were also in Java, on the east coast. We reckoned that a fast car could be over in an hour; we were in great danger. 'Hooky' and I were in the Consul's office in Tjilitjap discussing the best thing to do. Our intention was to acquire a craft of some kind. Suddenly, the Dutch skipper of a local coaster burst into the office crying out that his ship had been bombed to hell on the way into port and his crew, all Javanese, had fled as soon as the ship tied up. 'Only the chief engineer and myself are aboard,' he cried, 'I want some crew!' 'Crew? Crew?' we said, 'We are crew'. Those of our party rated as stokers went to the engine-room, but it was a coal-burning ship and our naval stokers had never shovelled coal in their lives. I am told it is a great art. They could scarcely get the fire hot enough to warm the water let alone get pressure up. The engineer was hopping mad. At last there was enough power to move. We let go and found our slow stokers had saved us: there had been a couple of submarines lying off the harbour which had sunk ships that had left earlier. The submarines had given up waiting for us and gone away. We slowly steamed to Fremantle, arriving there early in March 1942, about three weeks after the start of our escape.

In Fremantle we reported to naval authorities. I was sent to Melbourne to await instructions and, after a week, found myself posted to Mombasa to serve as Fleet Mine-sweeping Officer, Eastern Fleet, on the staff of Admiral Sir James Somerville. The headquarters of the Eastern Fleet were shifted to Colombo in autumn 1943 and the harbours at Colombo and Trincomalee were over-full. A separate port was needed for the small ships of the mine-sweeping base and I was given the job of finding one. I was flying as a passenger in an aeroplane over to India, when I sighted a tidal dock — just what we were looking for. I came back to Colombo and told Admiral Somerville. He sent for the Staff Navigating Officer who had a look at his chart and said, 'There is no such place!' I assured him there was — I had seen it. He and I went to have a look at it. It was a very fine private dock at Mandapan, Ceylon, owned by the Indian railway and was where their ferries for the India/Ceylon Channel docked and were re-fitted. The dock staff were very helpful and it became the mine-sweepers' base. I named the base HMS *Burong*, (Malay for 'bird'), inspired by my first bird's-eye view of it.

Then there was the question of appointing a new Commander Mine-Sweepers Bay of Bengal, a sea-going appointment. I told Admiral Somerville that I knew just the chap. 'Who?' he asked. 'Me, sir,' I said. He was rather surprised, but I was given the appointment and was very pleased to have another half-stripe.

I went to take over in Calcutta in the early summer of 1944 and found a flotilla of BYMS (British Yard Mine-Sweepers) swinging round their anchors, some in a run-down state. They were beautiful little American-built wooden ships; almost everything was electric — even cooking equipment — and had stamped on it: 'In case of trouble do not tamper, replace.' However, we had few spare parts and it was difficult to get any work done; the yards were already overworked. Some of the ships had difficulty in raising their anchors, but they had boats falls and I instituted a drill whereby anchors were raised by hand using these purchases. It was a lot of work and at first not at all popular. The men became accustomed to doing it and I made the whole flotilla (not only the ships without power) do it as a drill; weighing anchor this way became something of a competition and with practice was done smartly. Eventually the windlasses were replaced.

The art of mine-sweeping lies in exact station-keeping, particularly difficult in strong tides and cross-currents. We were issued with an instrument like a small sextant for this, but I think in practice station-keeping was mostly done by eye-sight. You had to keep your distance both from the ship on your beam and the ship ahead of you. I kept the flotilla busy at exercises until this art was mastered.

The problem was to find a yard which would keep the ships in repair. I found a yard upriver from Calcutta, manned by a Scottish family, descendants of people who once built clipper ships that were used to smuggle opium into China. A road bridge had been erected downriver of them and the yard had fallen on hard times. Consequently they were more than ready to do the work. But the question was: could the BYMS get under the bridge? Everything was measured beforehand, then came the first try. We lowered the radio mast and the ship crept forward; a crowd gathered on the bridge in anticipation. Slowly we approached. The man sitting on the road bridge raised a flag when the clearance was right; it looked impossible. It still looked impossible up to the last few yards. We passed under the bridge unscathed. From then on, all the BYMS went to the yard for repair. Each time a crowd gathered to watch a ship hit the bridge, and each time they went away disappointed. The yard was awfully good to the officers and men and attended to our repairs. Of course, I had to get all this approved, but I do hope somebody paid the yard-owners for their work.

I did not have a particular ship under my command and so had no proper home, especially when in port. In Calcutta I made friends with two wealthy bachelors who owned an extensive house and suggested to them that I might have the use of a small guest wing. They thought this over, and agreed. 'But of course,' they said, 'you'll have to have your own staff. We have only thirteen, that's including the men who look after our three dogs, and they're all fully occupied in looking after us.' I employed a staff of two.

With the start of the Arakan campaign we shifted our base for the mine-sweepers to Chittagong but continued to use the same yard at Calcutta for repairs. In the monsoon it was hard on our small ships to take the open sea route from Chittagong to Calcutta, so I asked the head of the pilots about the possibility of an inshore route through the tributaries of the Delta. He thought it would be possible but difficult. He and I took one of the BYMS and, with a Hooghli pilot on board, picked up local pilots as we went from village to village and stream to stream. It could be done but it was impractical.

The capture of Rangoon was the culmination of the mine-sweeping campaign of Burma, and afterwards the mine-sweeping flotilla was dispersed for various jobs. I am proud to say that during our Burma campaign not one of the ships in the flotilla was lost. I have to thank the officers and men for their assistance and cooperation, their smartness, enthusiasm and high morale. I was awarded my third DSC and my name was mentioned in dispatches.

The war in Europe was now over, and a fleet order was issued saying that any officer over the age of fifty serving afloat could apply for demobilisation. I applied, but to my surpirse the answer came back 'not eligible'. Then I remembered the way I had shed a few years when I had joined up. What to do? I went to the Admiral's secretary and asked his advice. 'Easy enough, old boy,' he said, 'the Admiralty are always making mistakes. Reapply, and say you can back it up with a birth certificate.' I reapplied, was granted my demob and flown to England.

I wanted to get back to Malaya as soon as possible, but the shipping companies only laughed at me when I went to book an immediate passage out East. The waiting list was two years. My son (who had also won a DSC during the war) was about to leave for the Far East as navigating officer of a flotilla of Fleet mine-sweepers and he suggested that I might be able to make the passage as his captain's guest. I jumped at the idea. John happened to know that his captain was dining and dancing at the Savoy that evening. I jumped in a taxi and headed for the Savoy, where I found John's captain. I asked him if I could travel to the Far East as his guest. 'I'm delighted to have you, my dear chap,' he replied, and promptly wrote out the invitation on a Savoy menu card, the nearest thing to hand. The Admiralty approved.

Malaya and my rubber and oil palm plantations were in a terrible mess when I returned in the autumn of 1945. Many of my friends had died in captivity, many others were sick men. It was sad to hear how many labourers in the estates had been taken off to build the railway in Burma and had never come back.

I went ahead with the building of my yacht *Selamat* to another Harrison Butler design, the eight-ton 'Dream of Arden' with built-up topsides. I found that the builder I had long had in mind, a Chinese man known as Mac, was now working for a Danish estate on the Bernam River about forty miles north of Kampong Kuantan where I lived. The only means of transport was the river, so Mac ran a small shipyard for the building and maintenance of the estate's launches. I went to the estate manager and asked his permission to have *Selamat* built at his yard. 'On one condition,' he said, 'that you build a second yacht alongside for me. I've always wanted a yacht built but never known how to set about it.' The two yachts were built in the yard, but fitting them out was a real headache just after the war.

At that time I was working very hard as a visiting agent and re-building my own properties. Occasionally I would indulge myself by flying down to Singapore for some weekend racing in a Sydney six-teen-footer I had there (a class my friend Ned Holliday had introduced to the Club when he was Commodore of the RSYC). These Sydney sixteen-footers were wonderful to sail and had a 16ft. hull, a bowsprit the same length and a spinnaker pole that was so long it came in three sections like a fishing rod. There appeared to be no way of reefing, but there was a crew of six and as the breeze rose, a member of the crew went up on the side to sit the boat up. We took a colossal amount of water on board and one member of the crew was always bailing – that had to be someone very light. The answer was to take on a girl crew member and one of the nurses from the hospital used to come every weekend. One of the crew had the job of buying her dinner on Saturday night, then bringing her sailing and bailing on Sunday.

Selamat was to be shipped from Penang to Port Said and from there

I planned to sail her to England without a motor. However, I could not find a crew who had sufficient time to sail with me the full distance from Malaya to England. In the end it was a great rush to get *Selamat* ready as the ship on which she was booked was rescheduled to arrive in Penang a fortnight earlier than expected. The launching and stepping the mast were a great scramble; I bent the sails as *Selamat* was towed down the river by the company launch. Joined by my crew Geoffrey Knocker, I sailed the 200-mile passage to Penang, leaving *Selamat's* sister-ship *Chencharu* still needing the finishing touches. Twenty-four years later the sister-ships were side by side again, in Corfu.

I returned to Malaya several times in the next few years during the Emergency, as director and visiting agent of various companies. I made the passage by 'flying-boat', the only time that air travel has been comfortable. We travelled from London by coach, stopping somewhere on the Hog's Back for breakfast then took off from − I think − Southampton Water. Take-off and landing were always lovely and smooth, and in sheltered waters, such as the Nile at Cairo. The journey took five days and ended in Singapore. We never flew at night but stopped over at luxurious hotels. We must have been held up at Karachi on one passage because I went sailing there with some local boys, who had a most exciting boat, which had a plank as an outrigger. Instead of reefing, the boy went further and further out on the plank.

I sailed *Selamat* for several years without a motor, cruising the Brittany coast, the Scillies and the west coast of Ireland. I was proud to be at Queen Elizabeth II's Coronation Review. We were allotted a position with so many cables from here, so many from there. As we had no engine Margaret and I went out the night before to find our position and mark it with an anchor buoy. In the morning we sailed out and picked up the buoy smoothly. We felt so smug when others were trying frantically to find their marks. In the evening there was the most wonderful display of fireworks that I have ever seen. That night it blew like hell and Osborne Bay was so full of sheltering yachts that you could almost walk from one to another.

Then an engine was installed in *Selamat* and she rather ceased to be only a sailing ship. In 1956 she returned to the Mediterranean via the Midi Canal − a trip that was like sailing through a wine list. In the following twenty years I have had the usual adventures of a cruising man, including having my ship stolen, for the second time.

In 1966 *Selamat*, crewed by Mary Danby, headed for Istanbul. It was an interesting passage through the Dardanelles and the Sea of Marmara, a wonderful cruising area. We came to the busy waters of the Golden Horn, where ferries, loaded with passengers, relentlessly crossed and recrossed. *Selamat* was just passing one such vessel when he suddenly moved out from his berth. To avoid ramming him I went from full ahead to full astern; then the gear jammed in astern and I could not shift it. Nor did I have the power in astern to stem the tide and we just went round in circles. I felt an utter fool. Even though everyone was hollering at me, I could do nothing. At last a customs launch came and towed us to a berth.

I went ashore and found out that there was a yard further up the Bosphorus who would sort out the trouble. The son of the owner of the yard spoke very good English. They sent a launch to tow us but we made no progress against the strong tide – or rather, we made a little progress until we had to round a headland, where we stuck. So a second launch had to come and it took two of them to tow *Selamat* up through the Bosphorus to the yard on the edge of the Black Sea. Here we met with kindness itself and the owner and his son worked wonders. It turned out that, in his time, the father had been a sailor, and master of a small brig. After I had recounted my sailing ship experiencies they could not do enough for me.

Two years later we were sailing down from Yugoslavia towards Greece. We rolled easily southwards with a fine, following wind. Towards evening the wind fell away. The small island of Merlera, which lies close north of Corfu, was near at hand so I decided to go in and anchor for the night. By the time we had closed the island it was dark, but I carried on, intending to anchor in a sandy bay near the big lighthouse on the island, which gave me my position. Just as we were preparing to anchor in what I thought was three fathoms, *Selamat* went aground – hard and fast. Within seconds the big swell left by the wind caught us and turned the ship so that we lay broadside on to it, thumping heavily on the hard sand, with no tide to lift us off. We launched the dinghy – which filled up several times before I could get it away from the ship – and I struggled out to lay the kedge anchor. We took the warp to the halyard winch on the mast and hauled and heaved. After hours of work the ship was lying head on to the swell; by then it was around 0300. We went below, sank half a bottle of whisky and fell into our bunks; but I could not sleep and crept up on deck to see how the ship was standing up to the punishment. I watched the bright lights of a passing steamer move across the night sky. *Selamat* thumped again, then lifted as the swell of the ship rolled in. I dashed for the winch and as each swell came in I took in the slack on the kedge-warp. With every swell we moved and soon we were free. We weighed the kedge and motored thankfully away. Mary left *Selamat* in 1970 to marry my friend Hum Barton, and I was indeed fortunate in finding Wendy Funnell to replace her. I have sailed some thousands of miles with Wendy – not without adventure – cruising the Mediterranean.

This year I sold *Selamat*. My home and my companion of thirty years has gone, a separation demanded by my deteriorating eyesight and *anno domini*. Nonetheless, sailing has blessed me with many good friends and a wealth of wonderful memories.

KERYL'S CRUISE DOWN CHANNEL

by John Clark

We decided to go on a few days' cruise in July, having just completed fitting out. The weather was fine, with little wind, although when it did blow it was – of course – from the wrong quarter. We spent most of our time day-sailing out of Studland or sunbathing on the beaches there. We met a number of Club boats, made many new friends and can now fully endorse the sentiments expressed by Arthur Underhill in the lovely centenary card.

Our main cruise began with the Beaulieu meet, our first meet and great fun, a splendid way to get to know other members. I do not know any other club which shares this remarkable and enviable custom.

The Monday after the meet found us alone with out friends the Carrs with *Havfruen*. We parted in the mist; a light north-west breeze carried them to Cowes and us in the direction of Dartmouth and the autumn peace of Alderney. Three hours later we were deep-reefed and thankful just to stagger into Yarmouth (where I hope no one saw my dreadful landing-on). We sat it out there until the following weekend; even then we got nowhere. We couldn't get round Portland, we had blasts from the west, followed by patchy calm and then more blasts, this time from the east. The wind was neither strong nor persistent enough to get us anywhere.

Whenever the *Keryl* furls her beautiful white pinions, we have to call upon one of Henry Ford's early inventions, which stirs its ancient bones within its cavern each time its services are required; but like most elderly creatures it soon tires and returns to slumber and dream of the days of its youth. Many years ago, I began to realise what I had taken on when I was caught in a thick fog, with a contrary tide and with the big boys booming round me. That dates *Keryl*; very few modern ships use a siren in fog.

I digress. To return to my subject, there comes a time during such a cruise as ours, when to rely completely on such unsettled weather can cause problems in Mammon's mills.

To be brief: the Dorset coast was our cruise. And if anyone wants to avoid the sometimes pestilential port of Weymouth he will find that with an adequate ground tackle and a sensible dinghy, the road just outside the port is an excellent anchorage with a small tidal range.

DOWN CHANNEL: -
Bluebird sets sail for Bermuda
(*a phrase that conjures up thoughts of McMullen and RCC traditions*)

by Robin Riverdale

John Hilton, Howard Hilton's nephew, heading a team consisting of one man and three women of ages ranging from nineteen to twenty-six, had been working up *Bluebird* at Lymington for a month or more and was nearly ready to take her back to the States. They asked me to go down as channel pilot and, I think, had in mind a teach-in on handling *Bluebird* before they set out across the Atlantic. I had left *Bluebird* at Brussels in August 1978, almost with tears in my eyes at the thought that I might never sail in her again, and I naturally jumped at this chance, which seemed rather appropriate as I had first met *Bluebird* in Ireland and acting as channel pilot had sailed her back to Lymington in 1977.

I boarded in Poole and found the crew very friendly and extremely anxious to sail. It was blowing fresh from the west and we first had a reefing drill as I saw no fun of taking a reef in the mainsail in the dark in a dirty sea off St. Alban's Head, with wind Force 6 and a crew who had never done it before. We then left Poole and did some sail drill in the open, followed by a much-needed sounding and anchoring drill before we anchored in Swanage Bay. We sailed at 0330 to catch the tide and, once clear of St. Alban's Head, set out towards the middle of the channel, putting Portland right out of sight with a westerly wind about Force 5 freshening. We needed some engine to maintain speed and make good use of the fair tide. At 0900 we came about to make a long slant which fetched us up in the afternoon with a landfall on Start Point.

By that time we had had a gale warning and it seemed prudent to take *Bluebird* into Dartmouth. We secured to a fine old Spanish sailing ship, *Pasqual Flores*, and the owner and his wife made us welcome, which overcame the nightmare of an era when the concourse of yachts in every port leaves no room for a stranger. Today there is no welcome, no space and a charge of £6.50 for securing to another vessel for one night – a total contrast to my first entry in *Bluebird* in 1925, when there were few yachts and plenty of room and everything was free.

Tuesday, 31st July There were gale warnings for Thames, Dover, Wight, Portland, Plymouth, Sole, and the Irish Sea, generally westerly and so a dead head wind. The strategy was to do as many of the jobs as possible that would have had to have been done in Falmouth. We

49

went out to Start in the afternoon, with gusts of up to about Force 7, to see what it was like. The sea and the forecast indicated return, but before doing so I put the crew through a general heaving-to drill; then it was back to the welcome of the SS *Pasquale Flores*.

Wednesday, 1st August This was another mixed day and useful jobs were accomplished. The shipping forecast at 1400 maintained gale warnings for the Thames, Dover, Wight, but not for the West; wind force was 6/7 westerly decreasing later for Portland and Plymouth. However, there were also gale warnings for Biscay and Finistere but no indication of cause. We had a sporting chance and sailed for Falmouth.

The wind as forecast was westerly 6/7 and we found ourselves way out off the Start, sailing up to seven and a half knots on a dirty great sea with wind against the tide. *Bluebird* was magnificent: she had no heavy water on board and was not even very wet. We sailed on into the night and tacked out past the Eddystone; with the wind decreasing in the early morning, we worked along the coast and entered Falmouth at about 1330 on Thursday, 2nd August. We eventually anchored at Mylor Creek after taking in water at the town quay. I discovered that I could catch a train home on Friday, 3rd August.

In Falmouth were more memories. It was under the old tree in the corn field that I had gone to sleep after arriving, exhausted, in the first *Bluebird* in 1925. Then there were perhaps six vessels in Mylor Creek; now it is a considerable establishment with about five hundred yachts. All the same we had a friendly welcome from Roe and the knowledge that it was from here that Eric and Susan Hiscock had made their departure on their last voyage to New Zealand. I left *Bluebird* having given the splendid youngsters a great list of jobs to do before departure, an outline programme prepared from the Atlantic Routing charts, and also a tentative programme for the fifteen-year refit that John Hilton and his father (now retired) proposed to do. This was designed to bring *Bluebird* up to first-class order when she reached Seattle. She had passed survey with one small defect and all sound; no doubt with this treatment she could double her value and also look forward to a useful life for another fifteen or twenty years, something the 1939 *Bluebird* had done.

Bluebird escaped the great gale that struck the Fastnet race. It was a relief to receive a cable: 'Bluebird arrived Horta. All well. Thank you.' After *Bluebird* had sailed from the Azores, hurricanes David, Frederick and Gloria struck. *Bluebird* was hit by Gloria east and north of David and Frederick, but escaped the full fury without damage and made Bermuda safely with her young crew to complete her fifth Atlantic crossing.

TRIP TO MOROCCO

by Colin McMullen

In 1978 I started to plan a trip to North Russia and down through the White Sea and the canal to the Baltic, but after a nine-month delay a final *niet* was issued by the Russian Embassy. To my future crew's relief we decided to sail on a roughly reciprocal course to the south.

Saecwen is a 35ft. Saxon wooden sloop, fitted with a Volvo Penta MD2 engine, a Gunning self-steering gear and – this year – a new mainsail; like her sisters she is a wholesome cruising vessel.

On Friday, 29th June we left Lymington with my sister Louise de Mowbray (RCC) and Captain John Lamb (RCC) and had a good sail down to Plymouth via Lulworth and the Yealm river. A week later we left the Mayflower Marina, with Vice Admiral Sir Bill Crawford (RCC) and my sister Louise bound south. They had arrived at 1630 on Monday, 9th July and we planned to leave next morning; however, Jonathan Trafford called our attention to the fair wind and we were away by sunset. After a gentle sail across the Channel we finally beat up to Brest in a strong north-easterly wind, arriving alongside the free pontoon at 1800 on Wednesday, 11th July. We found this a convenient spot and next day, after obtaining a couple of spare belts for the engine from a large local spare-part depot, we set sail for Spain at 1630.

After passing through the Chenal de Toulinguet we cleared the Raz at dusk and headed across the bay with a fine north-westerly fair wind which varied in strength and direction as we went further south. Sometimes we were under a well rolled mainsail and No. 1 jib and at others, under all plain sail with the genoa; occasionally we were able to 'goose-wing'. It was generally fine sailing with northerly winds which increased in strength as we neared the Spanish coast.

By 1630 on Sunday, 15th July the wind was NE Force 6 so we lowered the mainsail and proceeded under No. 1 jib. We had obtained a good DF bearing of Cape Villano and at 0215 on 16th July, we sighted the light which was finally abeam at 0445. By this time the wind was up to Force 7.

It was a rough night when we passed Capes Villano and Finisterre but the wind gradually eased and we completed the day in a light wind under spinnaker. We finally motored inshore north of Islas Agudo to anchor in the dark in Ensenada de Barra at 2245 on 16th July, four days out from Brest and after a fine sail.

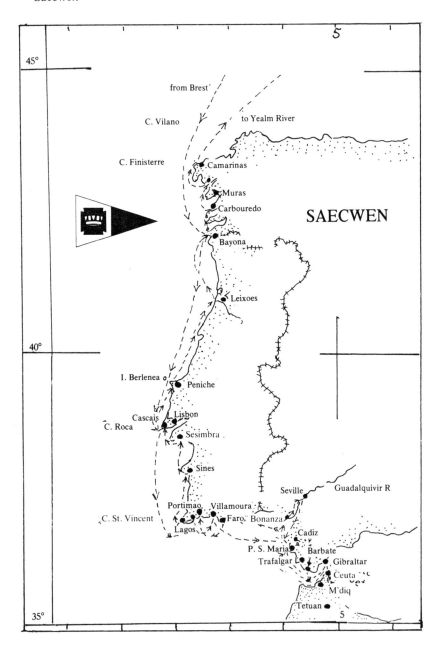

The next day, in a flat calm, we motored over to Bayona where we spent a very pleasant two days, during which we made the acquaintance of two charming Spanish Naval Officers and their families. They visited *Saecwen* and we visited their house ashore, where they were on holiday from Cadiz.

On Thursday, 19th July we were off again to the southward, passing *Luke's Minnie* (a fine old gaffer built by Luke in 1893), which was also just about to sail. We were soon well rolled down in a fine NW Force 5 and at sunset we handed the mainsail and sailed comfortably through the night under No. 1 jib, still making about five knots. The following day, again under all plain sail, we sighted Berlenga at 1245 and altered course to pass between it and Cape Carvoeiro. Sailing down this coast it became apparent that the Portuguese radio DF stations were not working properly, and this continued throughout the cruise. However, the Spanish stations on Capes Villano and Finisterre were broadcasting loud and clear.

As we passed Cape Roca, the wind gradually increased from the northward and by the time we approached Cascais, we were under a well rolled main and No. 2 jib. We entered the anchorage at 0250 and were surprised to find that *Luke's Minnie* was there before us. The next day the crew came aboard and we learned how well their long-keeled boat had run; but it had been hard work, with no self-steering gear, with muscle power continually required on a hard helm, and a long boom forever trailing in the following seas. However, we reckoned that as the total of their three ages was well under a hundred, they could take it. Our ages totalled rather more, so perhaps it was prudent for us to proceed a little more carefully!

We stayed a couple of days and then had another good sail with north-westerly winds, leaving Cascais at 0735 on Sunday, 22nd July and passing Cape St. Vincent at 1130 the next day. On the way I obtained a DF bearing of Sines, the only DF station along the entire Portuguese coast which seemed to be operating.

After rounding St. Vincent we sailed to the eastward and at 1615, anchored off the beach at Lagos, west of the harbour entrance. After a pleasant bathe the crew explored the town, while the skipper did likewise in the harbour under oars. Unfortunately we had underestimated the range of the tide and by the time we had all returned, *Saecwen* was grounded at low water, an incident of which I am not proud and which could have been serious if there had been a heavy swell. The following morning we unsuccessfully attempted to weigh the anchor; we finally broke it out by going ahead on the engine and set sail at 0600.

We decided to visit the new marina at Villamoura but as it did not appear on our chart, there was some confusion regarding its location. However, having found its latitude and longitude in the Light List, we had a dull sail, occasionally assisted by the engine, and entered

I. Berlenea
Peniche
Cascais
Lisbon
Sesimba
C. Roca
Sines
SAECWEN
Lagos Portimao
Villamoura
Faro
Bonanza
P. S. Maria
C. St. Vincent
Cadiz
Barbate
Gibraltar
Trafalgar
Ceuta
M'diq
Seville
Guadilquivir R.

CLOSE UP OF SOUTHERN TIP OF IBERIAN PENINSULA

10   5.

the harbour at 1715. Here we found a fully equipped marina, entered between two breakwaters and in an artificial dredged-out harbour. The only snag seemed to be the rather tedious filling in of numerous forms. When I had finally completed the forms, I was sternly presented with a printed warning. It immediately became the subject of a strict *Saecwen* Captain's Standing Order which I directed my crew to read carefully and initial. It read as follows:

AVISO

Por lei proibida a pratica de nudismo nas praias de Portugal

NOTICE

It is forbidden, by law, to practise nude sun-bathing on the beach

I am happy to report that no member of *Saecwen*'s crew disgraced our burgee in this way.

The following afternoon we left this rather dull but convenient marina and embarked on a frustrating, light weather, 97-mile sail to Cadiz. Even with the occasional help of the engine we did not arrive until two days later at 0815 on Friday, 27th July. We secured stern first to one of the pontoons in the Real Club Nautico de Cadiz with one of the clubs hauling-off ropes secured to the bow. These berths, although well sheltered by a small breakwater, are not easy to get into and the very recent building of a new short breakwater at right angles makes manoeuvring in this small but completely sheltered small yacht harbour very tight, especially in strong winds. The best thing is undoubtedly to go alongside something convenient and then seek help and directions from the marina office.

The yacht harbour is rather far from the shops and market; however, once we had mastered the drill for ringing up for a radio taxi, there were no problems, and we enjoyed our visit to this historic old town. We left at 0820 on Sunday, 29th July.

Once again we had a fair north-westerly wind, so we hoisted the spinnaker and passed close to Cape Trafalgar at 1520. However, by dusk the wind had dropped, but as we were in the straits, we motored into the Ensenada de Bolonia, anchoring in five fathoms at 2300.

I had a definite feeling of guilt at dropping the hook in the dark off the Spanish coast so near to Gibraltar for immediately after anchoring, I sighted a phantom darkened gunboat approaching us. However, my crew (who will testify that I was sober at the time) quickly put my mind at rest: it was an optical illusion created by a low star and a ship with few lights passing to seaward.

The next morning, Monday, 30th July, we were away at 0830 and after considerable help from the engine, we passed Tarifa. I think we were all thrilled when the fortress of Gibraltar came into sight. At 1500 we entered the harbour and secured in the pens but shortly afterwards were kindly moved by the QHM Commander Rogerson into the naval dockyard. We secured stern first to the wall in the Cormorant Camber.

So ended the first part of the cruise and on the whole it had been a splendid sail, with an RCC crew who, although perhaps a little elderly (we totalled 212), were so young in spirit and energy that it had been a happy trip. Bill and Louise now had to fly home. John Lamb rejoined the boat for the cruise to Seville, with Leila Wagstaff.

I found that our previous berth was unoccupied, so after securing stern first to the pontoon, we turned in. This was a mistake. At breakfast an extremely angry nightwatchman let it be known in no uncertain terms that we should have reported to him before mooring up.

I took a taxi to the Instituo Hidrografico to buy the chart of the Quadalquivir river but it seemed to have been withdrawn and I had no luck. I explained the problem to my taxi driver, who spoke English, and we went to a shop where I acquired a road map. After lunch we set sail, finally anchoring in the river just north of Bonanza at 2030, after a fine day's sailing in a Force 3/4 wind.

We had no problems entering the river, although there is considerable dredging activity on the bar, and we were fairly confident that we could reach Seville with the aid of FPIs and our map. After supper we were about to turn in, when two local officers of unknown authority arrived on board. They only spoke very rapid Spanish and we only had our English/Spanish dictionary. However, after an hour's prolonged discussion and negotiation, two bottles of whisky were exchanged for an excellent little pocket booklet chart of the river and with a final kissing of madame's hand, we parted *amigos*.

The next morning I put a bandage on the flexible exhaust pipe which had developed a slight leak; I was rather proud of this job which consisted of tin foil, encased in a sheet of lead, covered with a sheet of copper and secured with four jubilee clips. Although it did not completely cure the leak, it was acceptable and at 1000 we were away two hours before the start of the flood (as advised in FPIs). This worked well and although the first half of the river trip was under engine, we picked up a fine breeze in the afternoon and at 2000 entered the lock with no delay. We then passed through the commercial port and approached the Bascule bridge Alfonso XXI. It opened promptly and we berthed stern first to the Club Nautico, with an anchor out ahead, at 2045 on Tuesday, 7th August.

We spent two days in this delightful spot, which not only had the attractions of the beautiful city of Seville but also the excellent facilities of the Club Nautico, including its marvellous swimming pool.

At 0700 on Friday, 10th August we were away again. The bridge opened promptly, regardless of the rush hour, resulting in a large traffic jam. This (for us) efficiency may have been achieved by having climbed up to the control cabinet the day before, thanking the venerable gentleman, murmuring *manana* and pointing at my watch. As expected we missed the tide to the entrance of the river and after anchoring near No. 9 buoy at 1730 we passed *un nuit d'horreur* thanks to the flies and midges which we had not previously encountered. However, morale was restored the next day for after leaving the river on the ebb, we picked up a nice westerly breeze and then a strong easterly wind as we entered Puerto de Santa Maria, north of Cadiz, at 1830.

Looking back on our trip up the river, I was surprised at the number of sea-going ships we had passed of sizes up to about 10,000 DWT. It was also interesting that navigation by night was frequent; the pilots must be very able.

We enjoyed our short visit to Puerto de Santa Maria, which seemed more friendly than the rather impersonal Cadiz Marina; although at first sight it is even more difficult to moor in than at Cadiz. However, if one goes straight alongside the club pontoon on arrival, there are no problems. One of the Club sailors will board the boat and help to secure a four-point mooring. This is necessary because of the narrowness of the river and the fast-running tidal stream. One then uses the fog-horn to summon one of the Club boats for transport ashore.

We only stayed one night and left at 1250, Sunday, 12th August. We retraced our route southwards in a light wind, which had increased to Force 5 ENE by 1700. We finally passed Cape Trafalgar at 2140, in ever-increasing wind conditions from the eastward; this was the start of a short unpleasant Levanter. We spent the night semi-hove-to, under a heavily rolled main with no jib, to the south of Barbate in a very rough short sea which was probably typical of the Straits of Gibraltar during a strong Levanter with the wind Force 7/8.

The wind eased in the morning and we tacked up into the lee of Tarifa, where we hove-to in a sudden wind increase. However, after a couple of hours there was again a slight easing and we started to tack towards Gibraltar. We started in half a gale but after about fifty tacks, the wind had completely disappeared and we finally motored gently across Gibraltar Bay at midnight to be greeted by one of the most splendid phosphorescent dolphin displays that I have ever seen.

So ended the second part of our cruise and we sadly said good-bye to John a couple of days later. Reinforcements arrived, however, in the shape of my grandson Charles Watson (aged seventeen) as mate, and Miranda Francis. On Saturday, 18th August the four of us left on a short mini-cruise to M'Diq in Morocco and then Ceuta, returning to Gib at the start of another Levanter with a fine fair wind, on Tuesday 21st August. In Gib the exhaust pipe was repaired by Blands shipyard, we then re-stored for the trip home. Sadly, Leila had to leave us. Saturday, 25th August, we left harbour at 0900, homeward bound.

At the start of our journey we had an ESE wind Force 4/5. We passed Cape Trafalgar, for the fourth time, at 1540 and held our wind until 1815, when it finally died. We then motored most of the way to

Cadiz, where we finally secured (also for the fourth time) at 0300. During our trip to the entrance of Faro harbour next day we had a nice WSW wind, which gradually died until by midnight, we were again under the engine. During the day Charles distinguished himself by catching an eight-pound blue shark, which the skipper despatched with the mole-grip.

By 0820 we were up to the entrance of Faro harbour and after an unsuccessful attempt to motor in against a strong ebb, we anchored outside near a coaster, until we entered the harbour later with a flood tide, this time under sail. We anchored close north of Ilha da Culatra, a perfectly sheltered overnight anchorage off a nice sandy beach; the only snag is the heavy traffic of fishing boats sailing to and from Olhao.

We had a peaceful night and went on our way in the morning, leaving the harbour at 0740 in a flat calm. It was a frustrating day, with light winds and a lot of engine. However, things cheered up when Charles caught a bonito and finally at tea time, a nice westerly breeze arrived, allowing us to have a fine sail up the coast to Portimao, where we tacked in between the breakwaters at 1945 on Wednesday, 29th August. We anchored during a magnificent sunset.

We greatly enjoyed Portimao, which I felt was one of the best places we had visited on this coast. We only motored up to the town to do the shopping and spent most of the time in the outer harbour, which is a delightful anchorage.

We decided to sail on Thursday evening, but to await the off-shore breeze. It was not until 0250, however, that we weighed and proceeded along the coast in an ever-increasing northerly wind and it soon became apparent that this was something more than an ordinary offshore wind. As we passed Lagos and approached Cape Sagres we had an exciting sail past numerous fishing boats with their confusing lights. By dawn we were down to No. 2 jib and six rolls, so we tacked into the bay east of Cape Sagres, described in FPIs. We anchored close to a German yacht at 0735 and here we spent twenty-four hours while we rode out a short, northerly near-gale. The holding ground in this bay appeared good and neither *Saecwen* nor the German yacht dragged, despite the violent squalls.

By Saturday morning the wind had eased, so we sailed out of the anchorage under a well-reefed main and tacked round Cape St. Vincent as we headed north. By 1830 the wind had again died and we were under engine for intermittent periods until we arrived at Sines the next morning. We motored past the vast, new breakwater, finally anchoring off the town to the east of the small fishing harbour at 1005 on Sunday, 2nd September.

The breakwater is part of a large new industrial complex and the flare from the new refinery could be seen from far away. Unfortunately the breakwater suffered great damage during a severe Atlantic storm last winter and this may prove a set-back to the overall plan.

When we landed we were a little disturbed to see the large number of Communist notices and graffiti which were far more prolific than in any other Portuguese town that we visited. It was here that Miranda, expert on birds, sighted a kingfisher skimming across the water, but probably her most interesting achievement had been earlier in the Straits of Gibraltar, when she pointed out thirty-five hen harriers on a migratory course for Africa.

In the evening the mate produced pancakes, a far more successful exercise than his afternoon's fishing which had drawn a blank. The next day we sailed northwards in light winds to Sesimbra, where we spent the night and then on again northwards, again with little wind, to Cascais, where we arrived at 1935 on Tuesday, 4th September.

It again blew hard northerly during the night, and this wind helped us on our way up to Lisbon the following morning. It died at about midday, when we entered the Doca do Boss Successo and with the permission of the local navy, secured alongside a Portuguese naval recreational yacht; this was most helpful as the basin was extremely crowded.

We stayed here four days, and left on Sunday afternoon, 9th September, with a new crew: Captain Basil Watson RN, late of HMS *Hermione* and William Nicholl as third hand. After a day in Cascais we left at dawn in thick weather and a moderate north-west wind; we tacked up the coast, going about on the ten-fathom line, and beat past Cape Roca at about 1000. It was still thick and as we tacked up the coast to the north, we made great use of the depth meter, until the wind went light at 1830. Then we started the engine and motor-sailed the rest of the way to Peniche, anchoring to the west of the western breakwater at 2345.

The next morning we entered this busy harbour and despite the large number of sea-going fishing vessels at anchor or on moorings, there was still plenty of room to anchor along with three other yachts. There are large works in progress inside the harbour, presumably for the fishing boats, and it will be interesting to see how this fascinating place develops. It has a considerable attraction with its extensive fortifications and is certainly a most convenient port of call.

After a day in harbour we made another dawn start in fairly thick fog, which cleared a couple of hours later as we rounded Cape Carvoeiro. There followed a frustrating trip up the coast to the northward in light variable winds and often poor visibility. We had left Peniche at 0545 on Thursday, 13th September but it was not until Saturday the 15th that we entered Leixoes harbour. Not only had we suffered from lack of wind but on Thursday night we also experienced heavy rain. As before on this coast we obtained no DF bearings, and the echo sounder again proved itself a wonderful instrument in the thick weather conditions that often prevailed.

We were generally confused as we approached Leixoes from the southward; the breakwater light had been swept away and the pulsating refinery flare in the distance appeared to have the characteristics of the red flashing ISO light which marks the entrance to Oporto. However, as there were fifteen ships anchored off the entrance to Leixoes, we were not deceived for long; we entered the yacht basin at 0500. There followed an excellent run ashore to Oporto, a fascinating old town, and as the river is almost empty of traffic, I think I would brave the bar in future (providing the weather was suitable) and anchor in the heart of Oporto in preference to the unattractive commercial Leixoes.

We set off the next day again with a light and variable wind and a lot of motoring. Just before dusk the engine stopped with a nasty 'clunk' and we discovered a large piece of discarded nylon net round the propeller. We spent an anxious night in light winds, with the boat almost out of business and carrying about twenty degrees of helm.

However, the following morning was again calm, so after blowing up the rubber dinghy, a diving party went into action and largely thanks to William's efforts, we managed to cut the net away from our propeller. During the day we had some breeze, but it petered out in the evening; we finally anchored in Bayona at 2125.

On Tuesday the 18th we met John Burnford (RCC) in *Hunza*. After we had had lunch together he murmured 'Well I'm off for a sail.' 'Where to?' I asked. 'Brazil, next stop Ascension!' he replied. He was sailing his boat out single-handed to Brazil, to turn her over to his son Michael for a year.

Our trip that afternoon was less ambitious. After watering and fuelling ship we had a lovely sail over to Islas Cies, where we spent the night, exploring the island the next day. We had another pleasant sail later that afternoon, when we passed under the lee of the attractive island of Ons, with its little village, church, and fields. Then we tacked to the west of Isla Salvora in a fine breeze. However, it died before sunset, so we motored into Corrubedo and anchored at 2040 among several lobster-pot floats, which some sportsman had laid right across the anchorage. The next day the wind behaved totally differently: we started north in light airs with a lot of motoring but completed the day with a splendid sail into Muros. We started by berthing alongside but then anchored to the north of the harbour near the slipway.

The large fishing boats which come into harbour every evening make the alongside berths inside the harbour almost impossible, and the anchorage outside is not very well sheltered and has quite a long fetch to the north and east.

That evening we dined in the Café Mirimar, where Angelo Sanadres, who speaks good English, ministered to our wants and put through our two telephone calls to England with great efficiency.

On the 21st we left and tacked to the northward in an ever-increasing northerly wind. At 1900 we decided to surrender after hearing Force 7 forecast for South Finisterre and Biscay; we retreated back to San Francisco Bay, where we anchored in pitch dark at 2130.

The next day the wind blew very freshly from the north. Gales were forecast for the area, so we decided to stay at anchor. It proved to be a good anchorage, probably much better than Muros in strong northerlies. During the forenoon we saw a fine sight as *Liemba*, flying her new RCC burgee, streamed past under jib in a Force 6/7 as she headed south and – ultimately – across the Atlantic.

We were away the following morning and had a splendid sail to windward, passing Cape Finisterre at 1605. However, at 2155 the wind dropped so we motored towards Camarinas, anchoring just north of the town at 0050, with no wind and an adverse current. Time was running out, so we again started early with no wind and a lot of motoring. We passed Cape Villano at 1145, on Monday, 24th September on what was to be a 7½-day trip across the bay.

We had planned to keep well clear and to the east of the shipping lanes and revisit Brest for Vino; but head winds caused the port tack to be very much a losing tack and the starboard tack kept on pushing us back into the steamer tracks. It was a frustrating crossing: wind was not only adverse but also very light and the visibility was generally poor, often down to a mile.

We gradually worked across the steamer tracks to the westward, so we decided to stay there and cut out Brest. Finally, when west of Ushant, we picked up a fine southerly breeze and swooped quickly across the Channel, picking up the Eddystone light in bad visibility at 1900 on Sunday, 30th September. By 2240 we were back alongside the Mayflower Marina. It may be of interest, with regard to Eddystone, that I could not (as in previous years) hear its radio beacon and in thick weather Plymouth still seems an awkward place to make without radar.

After a trip up the Yealm river we had a nice last sail from there to the Solent, securing alongside the Royal Lymington Yacht Club pontoon at 1840 on Friday, 5th October.

So ended *Saecwen*'s 1979 cruise over waters well known to many members. We found it a rewarding, exciting and enjoyable expedition. We cursed the lack of wind on our return up the Portuguese coast but we were probably fortunate in not having strong continual northerlies.

TABLE OF DISTANCES

Date 1979		Miles	Engine Hours
29/6	Lymington – Lulworth	34	1
30/6	Lulworth – R. Yealm	81	2
1/7	R. Yealm – Plymouth	5	½
9-11/7	Plymouth – Brest	150	4½
12-16/7	Brest – E. de Barra	426	3½
17/7	E. de Barra – Bayona	20	2
19-20/7	Bayona – Cascais	215	0
22-23/7	Cascais – Lagos	122	1½
24/7	Lagos – Villamoura	24	3½
25-27/7	Villamoura – Cadiz	97	7½
29/7	Cadiz – E. de Bolonia	86	4
30/7	E. de Bolonia – Gibraltar	28	3
4/8	Gibraltar – Barbate	36	3½
5-6/8	Barbate – Cadiz	39	6
6/8	Cadiz – Bonanza	29	½
7/8	Bonanza – Seville	45	6
10-11/8	Seville – P. de Santa Maria	74	11
12-13/8	P. de S. Maria – Gibraltar	73	4
18/8	Gibraltar – M'Diq	28	4½
20/8	M'Diq – Ceuta	17	0
21/8	Ceuta – Gibraltar	16	½
25-26/8	Gibraltar – Cadiz	69	6
27-28/8	Cadiz – Faro Harbour	86	3
29/8	Faro – Portimao	36	4
31/8	Portimao – C. Sagres Anchorage	22	0
1-2/9	C. Sagres – Sines	60	10
3/9	Sines – Sesimbra	34	3
4/9	Sesimbra – Cascais	25	6
5/9	Cascais – Lisbon	10	1
9/9	Lisbon – Cascais	10	2½
11/9	Cascais – Peniche	49	6½
13-15/9	Peniche – Leixoes	118	19
16-17/9	Leixoes – Bayona	64	10
18/9	Bayona – I. Cies	7	0
19/9	I. Cies – Corrubedo	25	4
20/9	Corrubedo – Muros	24	2
21/9	Muros – E. de. S. Francisco	3	½
23/9	E. de.S.Francisco – Camarinas	35	3½
24-30/9	Camarinas – Plymouth	490	8
2/10	Plymouth – R. Yealm	5	½
4-5/10	R. Yealm – Lymington	110	½
	Total Trip	2927	159

DISASTER AT THE MOUTH OF THE ELBE

by Robin Gardiner-Hill

My last job in the army was in Holland and for the three previous years, I had kept *Pentina II* in Hellevoetsluis because there is splendid week-end sailing in the Haringvliet and the Ooster Schelde. This port is also convenient for the sea lock at Stellendam so it is a good starting point for longer cruises. *Pentina II* was a Kings Amethyst 33ft. OA with an 8½ft. beam and 5½ft. draft. I had owned her since 1964, when she was built, and we had enjoyed cruising together every year after that. I thought that I knew her ways and I certainly loved her; indeed, being a bachelor, my friends often said that I was married to her. She was Bermudan cutter rigged and, in a wind of over Force 4, went to wind-ward best under a yankee jib and main with no staysail, a rig which I found delightfully simple to handle on my own. *Pentina II* had one of the early vertical-axis Aries self-steering gears and was somewhat underpowered with a very reliable Volvo Penta MD 1, which gave four and a half knots in good conditions.

I retired in the middle of the summer and moved aboard her, in-tending to sail to the Baltic for the rest of the summer. We left Helle-voetsluis by the 0800 bridge on 27th June and were in Borkum, by way of Sixhaven, Harlingen and Dokkum, by 2nd July.

We arrived in Borkum at 1530, in time to join the rush to buy fresh shrimps from a fishing boat which had just entered. Everyone in Borkum was helpful and friendly but I fear that I rather disappointed a customs officer who asked me whether I wanted my passport stamped. Un-thinkingly I replied: 'No, not particularly.' He explained that most English yachtsmen asked for a Borkum stamp in their passports, pre-sumably to prove that they had been in *Riddle of the Sands* country.

Local advice stated that it was best to go direct from Borkum to Cuxhaven and this I decided to do, although I now think I was wrong. Writing in the *Journal*, Dick Stevens, who admitted that he had been worried about leaving Cuxhaven bound westward, said that the answer was to call at Helgoland. In the light of bitter experience I would do this bound eastward and not leave Helgoland until conditions were highly suitable. It is so easy to be wise after the event.

At 0745 the next morning we left Borkum by the Riffgat to catch the first of the off-shore flood. There was quite a rough sea in a W Force 4 close in to the island, but the Riffgat itself presented no problems and there appeared to be plenty of water. After following the coastal buoyage up to the Accumer Ee, course was set for the Elbe 1 light-vessel. As dusk fell its light appeared, as did the main light on Helgoland. By 0030 on 4th July we were established in the well-buoyed Elbe channel; the wind was fair, NW Force 4/5 and the tide was just starting to make. Big-ship traffic was heavy and we were avoiding it by keeping well into the line of green-light buoys marking the starboard side of the channel. There was some swell and further on the channel bends to starboard in a more southerly direction which would have brought us on to a dead run. I had not visited Cuxhaven before and preferred not to reach it until dawn. With all these factors in mind, I decided to hand the main and run on gently with the flood tide under jib only. I therefore rounded up to port to hand the main. However, the main was stuck – presumably because a screw had worked loose in the track, although I shall never know for sure. I could only lower the main about two thirds of the way and we were effectively hove-to on the starboard tack and slowly fore-reaching southwards. Realising this I gybed, made some offing from the side of the channel and rounded up to try again. I did not go as far as I should have done because a nearby merchant ship was approaching. This time I made an error of judgement and struggled unsuccessfully with the stuck main too long. The result was that we drifted too far out of the channel and suddenly heeled over to an extreme angle, running well and truly aground on the edge of the Scharhörn Riff. Our position was about 53° 59' N 08° 23' E; this can be clearly seen on German chart no. 44, which shows just how steep the bank is very close to the buoyed channel. The area is marked *zahlreiche Wrackreste* and I regret that I have made the wrecks even more numerous.

I immediately laid out my 35lb CQR anchor and twenty fathoms of chain and handed the jib. I was still unable to lower the main completely but lashed it to produce minimum windage. I confess that I was not very worried: there were still five hours of tide to rise, the anchor was holding and I thought that I could wait for the tide to lift her off and then recover the anchor under engine. About an hour later the tide had risen enough to keep *Pentina II* afloat most of the time, but she was bumping and a heavy surge had built up over the bank. The engine was running full ahead and the chain was snatching violently. Suddenly I heard a loud bang and found that the chain had sheared the port samson post off at deck level. With some difficulty I resecured the chain to the starboard samson post, having veered more chain to give a better catenary. Half an hour later we were again in heavy surf and pounding badly when the second samson post sheared in the same way as the first. The chain ran out and was lost; it parted the bitter-end lashing in the chain locker and the whipping end cut the lower starboard lifeline.

The situation was now serious: we were losing ground on to the bank, the engine was not really helping much—although I kept it running all the time—and the pounding was very bad indeed. As always on such occasions the wind was increasing or at least seemed to be (I doubt that it was ever really more than Force 6) and we were, of course, on a lee shore. Clearly the time had come to sink one's pride and let off distress flares.

Despite the heavy traffic in the estuary it was about an hour before I made contact with a ship; by that time I was down to mini-flares and flashing with a torch. I cannot really say that mini-flares are better than rockets and hand-held flares, but they produced results. My flashed SOS was finally acknowledged. Many ships had passed and I think the problem was that in a busy channel like this, they are far too busy looking for their marks and at other ships – to say nothing of the radar – to notice what is happening abeam, well out of the channel.

I now knew that rescue would be only a matter of time but the incessant pounding made things very difficult. Fortunately I had two very thick kapok cockpit cushions and most of the time managed to keep one of these underneath me; I think that this probably saved me from serious injury. I did, however, suffer two cracked ribs and sitting down was uncomfortable for some weeks afterwards; in addition, below the waist, my body was more black and blue than white. I was also soaked through but not really cold – there was always plenty to do. At one point I went below to make up an emergency bag containing ship's papers, passport, wallet, chequebook and so forth, but I was worried about doing this as several stainless steel bottle-screws had parted, the mast – which was stepped on deck – was rocking through quite an angle and I was afraid that it might fall on the dog house and trap me below. The cabin was a sad sight with oily bilge water everywhere.

As dawn broke it was possible to see how far we had been carried down on to the shelf and we were now about half a mile south of Scharhörn Beacon (approximately 53° 58′ N 08° 24′ E) but at high water still about a mile from the Island of Scharhörn. At about 0600 there was the welcome sight of an approaching lifeboat but it could not get within half a mile; they launched their *Tochterboot*, a shallow draft skimmer carried on the afterdeck, which appears to have a powerful engine and carries a crew of two. Shallow water prevented it from sailing round on to my lee side. Handled with great skill it made one or two trial runs with a bows on approach, during which I handed over my emergency bag. They shouted to me to climb out over the lifelines – not an easy task as we were heeled over and still pounding. The *Tochterboot* has a steel post forward, against which the crew member braces himself with both arms free and outstretched. On the next run I was able to jump for it and was caught in his arms. While the boat backed off, he opened a forehatch and I was bundled below; it was rather claustrophobic with no head-room but at least there was a bunk to lie on.

Later there was much banging as the *Tocherboot* was taken back on board the main lifeboat. I was let out, stripped and shown to a bunk. The lifeboat turned out to be the SK *Arwed Emminghaus* from Cuxhaven. The captain (not the coxswain as at home) was Carsten Hoffman whose father had also been captain of the lifeboat. *Arwed Emminghaus* is superbly equipped and all the crew members, except the doctor, are full-time professionals. I was given a very thorough medical check up and had to suppress a feeling that they were a little disappointed at not having to use some of the more elaborate medical equipment.

The harbour police boarded at Cuxhaven but were friendly and easily satisfied and I fell into the excellent hands of Doktor Meinhard Kohfahl. He is the part-time lifeboat doctor, a qualified lifeboat crew member, a highly experienced cruising yachtsman, an officer of the yacht club, the Port Medical Officer as well, it seems, as many other things in Cuxhaven. He took me to his home and organised everything while I slept until lunch-time. Over lunch Meinhard explained to me that there was a survey crew working on the Island of Neuwerk and that at low water they would go in their four-wheel drive vehicles across the sands to Scharhörn and save as much of my gear as they could. At the evening high water we would travel out to Neuwerk in the lifeboat and collect the gear. This was good news indeed. Meinhard also told me that the local newspaper had telephoned to ask whether I wished to sell my story to them. I declined the invitation, but this may have been a mistake: I read a highly coloured account the next day, which claimed I had been rescued at the last moment from my 13-metre yacht, having lost my way in a severe north-westerly storm. Everything had been exaggerated. However, the report was read by the British Consulate in Hamburg and they kindly rang up to see if I needed assistance. I was able to assure them that I was being looked after superbly.

At about 1700 Meinhard and I drove down to the lifeboat and we went out to Neuwerk, following the broomed channel to the tiny harbour. It soon appeared that the survey crew had done sterling work and saved over three quarters of my gear and belongings. Everyone set to work transferring them to the lifeboat and the salvage claim was promptly settled with a case of beer — of which there appeared to be a copious supply on board the lifeboat. On the way back, over some of the plentiful beer and with Meinhard interpreting, I had a long conversation with the lifeboat captain. He told me that flares should always be let off in pairs with an interval of about ten seconds. Otherwise someone sees what might or might not be a distress flare, watches for a bit and if he does not see another, tends to assume that it was only his imagination. I am sure that this is sound advice but from my experience it is not too easy to follow. When one is being thrown about and, most of the time hanging on with one hand, it takes quite a long time to prepare and let off a flare — especially in the dark.

On its return to Cuxhaven the lifeboat went round to the Alter Fischerihafen, where my gear was off-loaded into the yacht club's winter laying-up shed. Meinhard assured me that I was welcome to stay with them for as long as I liked and asked if I had decided yet what I was going to do next; I replied that I would go back to England to find another boat. He told me that there were two boats for sale in the Cuxhaven Yacht Club and suggested that I had a look at them. I said that I was far too tired to make any decision that night, but my excuse was dismissed as irrelevant. We went to the Club where there was just enough daylight to make out a pretty little 29ft. steel-hulled sloop with a marked sheer-line and a teak deck. *Lorbas* had entered my life. Over a drink in her snug cabin I fixed up with Peter, the owner, to have a trial sail in her the following Saturday.

The next few days were tedious. I had to write reports on the loss of *Pentina II*, return ensign warrants and so on, as well as listing and sorting out all the gear that had been recovered and trying to save anything that was still of any use. It had all been soaked in salt water and much of it in oil as well. Frau Kohfahl very nobly washed out everything that was washable. Jürgen Hiort was also a great help in dealing with the local insurance representatives and so forth, while many members of the Cuxhaven Yacht Club also came to my aid in various ways. One evening as we were sitting on his boat in the Club marina, Meinhard remarked: 'Now what do you need? If we just sit here the person who can deal with it will come by.' In this way problems that varied from getting my spectacles repaired to finding a solicitor simply disappeared. I was asked to write something in the Club visitors' book and put: 'If you have to be shipwrecked this must be the best place in the world for the purpose.' Two days after the wreck, the lifeboat went to have a look and reported that not one piece of timber larger than a metre was left.

I had borrowed the keys to *Lorbas* so I could have a very careful look at her on my own; the more I saw of her the more I liked her. She is 29ft. OA, 8¾ft. beam and 4½ft. draft, and 7¾ tons Thames. The mast is stepped in a tabernacle and can be lowered, which is particularly useful in Holland. She has a long, straight keel and is directionally stable. We had our trial sail in a Force 6 and she behaved well. The steel hull had been built by Assmann of Norddeich, and Peter, who is an engineer, had finished her himself and done a very fine job. The teak deck is laid over steel and (something that particularly appealed to me in view of my recent experience) the three samson posts are large and made of steel clad with teak. She has a Saab diesel which gives six knots.

Peter obviously had the building bug and had just finished another boat, thus owning two. He was anxious to sell and I was anxious to buy so matters were concluded speedily and *Lorbas* became mine. I had intended to call her *Pentina III* but Meinhard and others talked me out of it on the grounds that it was unlucky and that *Lorbas* was a nice name anyway. I found out that it is a Prussian dialect word for a very lively, small boy who is always busy with his own affairs. I fitted her (or him—my son?) with a Sharp tillermaster and made several minor modifications to suit single-handed cruising.

On 19th July I called on the lifeboat to bid the crew farewell and top up their beer supplies. This proved to be rather dangerous as every member of the crew appeared to have his own bottle, each containing a different kind of *schnapps*, all of which I had to try. I rashly told them that I was leaving at 0715 in the morning to catch the tide up to Brunsbüttel Koog and the Kiel Canal; they were also bound for Brunsbüttel in the morning and would doubtless see me on my way. Laden with gifts from Cuxhaven (including the yacht club burgee) and a new log book from Meinhard, I embarked in *Lorbas* and turned in early.

The morning of 20th July dawned. There was a drizzle blown up the estuary by a brisk W Force 5/6 and I have seldom felt more like turning over and going back to sleep. However, I was shamed into leaving by my ill-advised remarks in the lifeboat the previous day. Halfway to Brunsbüttel the lifeboat came up astern. Much hooting and waving followed, to the complete mystification of several other yachts nearby.

From then on, my cruise was quite normal: at times enjoyable, frustrating, exhilarating and even faintly frightening. It was cruising as we know and love it.

FROM THE BALTIC TO THE MED IN *QUICKSILVER*

by Arthur Beiser

A sailor disregards omens at his peril. No omens could be clearer than the snow that fell when *Quicksilver* was launched early in May or the fog that attended her rigging the following day. Obstinately we persisted in our plans, which were to proceed from Copenhagen to Ile des Embiez in the South of France, northabout via Norway, the Shetland and Orkney Islands, Scotland, and Ireland, instead of taking the shorter route via the English Channel. We had had miserable weather the previous summer and only a paranoiac would have anticipated worse the following year. Even so, there we had a great deal of pleasure; and the almost total absence of other yachts (under wiser command) in the northern waters was a welcome change from the crowds in the Baltic and Mediterranean where we usually sail.

Quicksilver is a centreboard version Swan 47, designed by Sparkman & Stephens and built by Nautor in Finland in 1978. Her first season was spent in the Baltic, our tenth cruise there over the years, and when we left Copenhagen on 23rd May, we looked forward to stretching her legs in the greater waters ahead. We were four at this point: Juliet and Jim Rickards (RCC), my wife Germaine, and myself. A robust south-easterly pushed us north in fine style to Helsingør, and when it eased after lunch we set the spinnaker. The sun came out, but late in the afternoon the wind vanished and we motored the last of the seventy-two miles to the island of Anholt. Barely a dozen yachts were in the harbour, in contrast to the two hundred plus we had found there the previous August.

Usually we stay for a few days, sometimes a week or two, when we visit Anholt, so we can enjoy its miles of clean beach and its wild interior. However, the next day's chill drizzle was hardly beach weather and instead of enjoying a morning swim, we donned long underwear and oilies. After a chat with the friendly harbour-master and the purchase of a large cod from a fishing boat, we left close-hauled in a NW Force 4, headed for Hals at the entrance to Limfjord. In the afternoon the wind eased and veered to the north, so we replaced the jib with the MPS (multi-purpose spinnaker), which is a cross between a drifter and a spinnaker. Set flying tacked to the stemhead with no pole, the MPS is naturally easier to cope with than the true spinnaker we had set the day before; it is less effective, however, with the wind well aft. But the MPS gives a mighty push on a reach, and its red and yellow

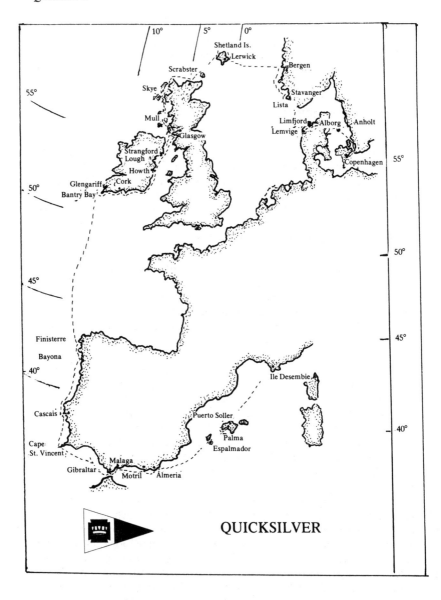

QUICKSILVER

stripes cheered up an otherwise grey day. We sighted Hals Barre light-house at 1730 and took in the MPS when we got there, running the rest of the way to Hals in a rising wind under main alone. We tied up alongside a quay in the small harbour and, at 1930, sat down to a feast of baked cod.

Limfjord cuts across the northern end of Jutland and, for a west-ward passage, provides a protected alternative to the open Skagerrak. The vigorous south-westerlies of the next few days confirmed the wisdom of this choice of route. Germaine and I found the low, nearly featureless landscape, relieved blankly only by staring cattle, as mono-tonous as on a previous crossing; but this time the trip was enlivened by the discovery of a new highway bridge at Glyngøre, just past Ny-køping on the island of Mors. The bridge was not shown on my recently purchased Danish chart of Limfjord; nor was its overhead clearance marked on the structure as is the case with some other Danish bridges. Passing boats gave widely varying figures for the clearance, so I called Skagen Radio by VHF. After a while the operator came up with twenty-eight metres as the magic number, well in excess of the twenty-two metres we need. We passed under the bridge to anchor all alone in the Lysen Bredning nearby.

The following day we took advantage of a Force 5 wind in these sheltered waters to practise reefing the working jib. This involves shifting to a new clew and tack a few feet above the normal ones, and then tying up the bunt of cloth. This process is easier than changing to a smaller jib (the jib's normal area is 560^2 ft., and the reef reduces this by a third to 366^2 ft.), and when reefed it will work nicely in collaboration with the reefed main with or without the fore-staysail. Indeed, the reefed jib alone gave *Quicksilver* five knots at forty degrees off the apparent wind that day. Just after lunch we tied up in Lemvig, a pleasant town a few miles south of the Thyborøn channel to the North Sea.

The weather was rotten throughout the next two days, with squalls of up to Force 8 interspersed with thick fog, and we were grateful for the facilities offered by the marina and the adjacent holiday camp; these included a sauna and a heated swimming pool, both welcome after the cold and damp of the previous week. Finally, on 31st May, the weather became more settled and the forecast for a passage to Norway less pessimistic. A warm south-easterly greeted us outside the harbour when we left, late in the afternoon, and we had a fast, joyous run up to Thyborøn and out into the North Sea, under main and the large, reaching jib.

By midnight the wind had gone entirely and at 0630 a heavy fog reduced visibility to about fifty metres. Eventually a light, flukey breeze came up that shifted around between south-east and north-east; but we gladly accepted constant sail trimming in exchange for turning off the engine so that we could listen for shipping. With the

help of the RDF, we located the Lista lighthouse on Norway's southern
tip and by noon we were close enough to hear the twin blasts of its fog
signal every ninety seconds. We slowly headed inshore under power in
the hope of seeing land before we ran out of water. We soon spotted
the remains of a coaster and a fishing boat, both wrecked on some
reefs. For some reason these wrecks upset the others, but I kept on and
was rewarded by the appearance of a lighthouse dead ahead in the mist.
While we were looking up the Lista lighthouse as a check, our lighthouse
suddenly stood up, reeled in its fishing line, and walked away. It had
been a fisherman wearing a conical hat. We were right at the entrance
to Lista harbour, a mile or so away from the lighthouse itself, and we
went inside and anchored to await better visibility.

The fog did not clear until the next morning, and even then a menacing bank of it stood not far off-shore. The wind was Force 2 from the
north-west and in view of the lurking fog, we motored the forty-one
miles up the coast to the small fishing port of Sirevaag. As on our 1972
visit there in *Minots Light*, Germaine and I were struck by the somno-
lence of the place: except during working hours (and not often then),
nobody appeared on the streets or quays, nobody was to be seen in
the gardens of the houses, and only the odd car suggested it was anything other than a ghost town. The only living thing to notice our
presence this time was a cat, to which Germaine presented the remains
of our dinner of poached halibut.

There were squally showers in the morning that subsided by noon
and we spent the afternoon sailing up to Tananger, where we tied
alongside the new breakwater. A flat calm the day after persuaded us
to stay in Tananger to catch up on odd jobs and stretch our legs ashore.
On Tuesday we were favoured with a light easterly – not a common
wind in those parts – and we sailed north through Karm Sound, past
the busy towns of Kopervik and Haugesund. In the early evening we
put into Espervaer, a small harbour that is handsomely situated inside
a group of islands just west of Bomlakuk. A large cormorant with its
wings apart was perched on a rock at the southern entrance. It seemed
to be regarding us with great interest; closer inspection revealed that
the cormorant was a silhouette cut from sheet metal and painted black.
We made fast to a quay, where we found diesel oil and water and despite the later hour, we were able to top up *Quicksilver*'s tanks. After
dinner we wandered around the village but, as in Sirevaag, we found
few signs of life among the several dozen well-kept houses that were
scattered about.

The shipping forecast at 0625 on Wednesday was benign, reporting
a weak low over the entire North Sea with nothing much in the way
of wind; we left Espervaer shortly after. Although we had visited a
few new harbours, our route from Copenhagen had covered waters
with which Germaine and I were familiar from earlier cruises. Now
we were off to the Shetlands – which were new to all of us – with

the added spice of a North Sea passage. But the day did not match our excitement; the sky was flat, calm and overcast. For twelve hours we motored across a glassy sea until finally a NE Force 3 came up. We gratefully set the main and reacher and *Quicksilver*, equally pleased, began to lope along at six or seven knots. There was fog not far behind the wind, however, and shortly, visibility was down to perhaps a quarter of a mile. A damp, cold, anxious night followed. The anxiety was not about navigation — I was able to supplement the DR plot with RDF lines of position, various depth contours, and the fog signal of the Frigg gas platform — but the fact that a radar reflector, even if correctly oriented (most are not), is no substitute for a radar itself. I am sure I would not miss a radar so much at times like this if I had not had one for nine years on *Minots Light*, *Quicksilver*'s predecessor. That night we all spent a lot of time — without success — trying to figure out a way to mount a radar scanner on *Quicksilver* without spoiling either her sailing ability or her appearance.

The fog was still with us at 1345 when, to our great relief, there appeared to port a triangular shadow whose form matched that shown in the *Pilot* for Noss Island (just east of Mainland, Shetland's main island). That we had hit Noss on the nose was confirmed by the gannets, guillemots, kittiwakes, fulmars, and puffins that flocked from the island to inspect us. Noss is a favourite nesting place for sea-birds and, as navigator, I waited in vain for congratulations as the others busily identified the birds that wheeled around us. I have always been uneasy around sea-birds since learning that Aeschylus was killed when a gull dropped a turtle on him, after mistaking his bald head for a stone on which to crack its shell open. Of course, there was nothing to fear on this occasion; I had not ventured outside without a woollen hat since Copenhagen (nor would I for a long time to come).

We felt our way round to Bressey Sound, where visibility was better, and then ran up to Lerwick. We entered the small boat harbour and tied up with the help of the uniformed assistant harbour-master, who took our lines. After we were secure, lines coiled, fenders and fender boards in place, and the engine off, I climbed up to thank him. 'No trouble, no trouble,' he said, 'but you can't lie there.' A quarter of a century's cruising has taught me self-control in such situations; I silently counted to ten and then asked him where we should go. He pointed to the inner corner of the nearby Albert Dock, where we finally made fast. Two amiable customs officers quickly arrived and when the paperwork was done, we relaxed with some much-needed refreshment and learned from them about life in Shetland. Both were 'sooth moothers' (newcomers to Shetland always arrive via the south mouth of the harbour), one from Liverpool and the other from Barra; both were happy in Lerwick despite its climate and remoteness.

The next day, we enjoyed our exploration of Lerwick and found the people charming and the prices a great improvement on those of

Quicksilver

Norway. After lunch on Saturday we managed to extricate *Quicksilver* from the fishing boats that were tied up two and three deep around us and headed north to Yell Sound. No trees interrupted the smooth, rounded contours of the islands, and the occasional stone house stood out starkly. Everything was green, sometimes spotted with white sheep. It was spare, understated landscape, not without a certain attraction. At 1700 we anchored at the head of Boatsroom Voe, a narrow bay at the south-east end of Yell Sound. The temperature was 10°C and we kept the cabin heater on while we enjoyed four fine steaks that Juliet and Jim had bought in Lerwick. It seemed strange to be living so well in such a bleak silent corner of the world, sipping wine, eating ice cream for dessert and listening to a Bach tape afterwards. Cold beans from a can eaten with a spoon gripped by gloved hands would have been more in keeping with the spirit of the place.

Strong currents run between the Shetland Islands and we stayed at anchor until slack water at 1145. Then, with a fair current to supplement a south-west wind, we sped up Yell Sound. From the fairway the only sign of the oil terminal at Sullom Voe was an extensive housing estate nearby. At the northern end of the Sound we turned west inside Gruney Island and then south-west, giving us a beat past the fine red cliffs of the Mainland coast. In St. Magnus Bay the rain that had been threatening all day poured down and we were delighted to reach the island of Papa Stour in the early evening. Three seals watched us anchor in Housa Voe, a pretty place, and the inhabitants of the few houses there waved to us in greeting.

We woke to sunshine and left Hausa Voe for Orkney under power in a flat calm. We chugged along over a glassy sea all day; near Orkney we passed a French ketch: only the third cruising yacht we had seen since leaving Denmark. We anchored between Eday and Calf of Eday, needing five tries before the CQR found a patch clear of thick weed on the sand bottom. By the time we were secure, the roast leg of lamb was overdone and Germaine was in a bad mood.

Heavy fog greeted us in the morning, but visibility improved to a mile or two by midday, adequate for a run to Stromness on the south-west corner of Mainland, Orkney's chief island. It was another windless day, and we motored up Westray Firth and then down the Mainland coast. A fog bank blocked Hoy Sound where Stromness lies, and we decided to continue on to Thurso Bay on the mainland instead of trying to make Stromness blind. Again I wished we had had a radar. However, Thurso Bay is a good target in fog: it is four miles wide with a lighthouse at either end, each with a distinctive sound signal; furthermore it is clear of the Merry Men of May tide-race. We figured that once we picked up one or the other of the signals – a siren at Dunnet Head on the east, a horn at Little Head on the west – we could proceed using echo soundings as a guide to an anchorage. On we went towards yet another fog-shrouded landfall, with regular RDF checks when we reached the Pentland Firth and its strong tidal streams. The triple blasts of Dunnet Head's siren came in as expected, and we proceeded along the forty-metre contour towards Dunnet Bay (the south-east corner of Thurso Bay), a few miles away. After an hour, however, the siren seemed to have the same bearing and to be just as loud, and an RDF fix placed us in the same position as before: we had expected some adverse stream along the west side of Dunnet Head, but not one of seven knots. We were cold, damp, tired and far from happy with the increasing darkness to cope with as well as the fog. We turned west to escape the worst of the north-going stream, which meant losing the security of the well defined forty-metre contour. After going two miles on the log, which meant perhaps half that over the bottom, we turned south and soon picked up the forty-metre contour again, this time in a weaker stream. We followed the contour until it turned west, which signified that we were in the mouth of Dunnet Bay, and then went south-east until the water shoaled to ten metres, and then anchored. Visibility was still less than a boat length. It was now midnight; we were suddenly starving and Juliet's scrambled eggs were most welcome.

At daybreak the fog had disappeared and it was good to see that we were anchored where we thought we should be. After breakfast we went over to Scrabster harbour and tied to the fish-market pier. The harbour is no longer used very much and we were able to remain alongside while we waited for good weather before we rounded Cape Wrath. Juliet and Jim had to leave the following day, so Germaine and I were on our own. Scrabster is not a very prepossessing place, but it does have a cordial harbour-master and a fair restaurant, and it is not far from the larger Thurso, whose shops and launderette took care of our needs. A local RCC member, Wing Commander Mackie, saw our burgee while he was driving past and came over with greetings, some crabs and an avocado for us, which we greatly appreciated.

Several days of ominous weather forecasts kept us in the harbour. Cape Wrath gets its name from the Norse word *hvarf* (turning point); it is hardly in the same league as Cape Horn but we wanted reasonable conditions before we tackled it. But the winds that did come on those days were nowhere near as strong as the predicted SW Force 6 and we finally left Scrabster on 19th June despite the continuing pessimism of the forecasters. The winds were light and variable and we had an uneventful passage round Cape Wrath and down to Loch Laxford. The coast westward to Cape Wrath seemed rather bleak but once we were round the corner, the scenery improved and Loch Laxford itself provided dramatic views in all directions. We anchored in Loch A'-Chadh-Fi, a lovely spot where the air is scented and only birdsong breaks the evening stillness. Germaine had anticipated a late arrival and cooked a chicken the day before. Dinner was ready by the time I had tidied up on deck.

The next day's forecast included gale warnings for area Hebrides, so instead of leaving, Germaine and I inflated the dinghy and went over to Ardmore. There was no gale however, only zephyrs; but at midnight a clap of wind heeled *Quicksilver* over and a Force 7 continued all night. The 0625 forecast was cancelled because the forecasters were on strike, but the newsreader did say that gales were expected in all northern sea areas; the wind was still blowing so we stayed put for another day. We did not regret this chance to enjoy each other's company and to unwind, away from the shore and other people. The cruise so far had not been quite what we had hoped it to be – largely due to the weather – and we were pleased at the prospect of soon getting rid of our long underwear. (I regret to say that this did not happen until mid-July in Ireland.) Finally the weather became fair and we made our way south to the Summer Isles and then to the Isle of Ewe in Loch Ewe.

A north-westerly the next day made anchoring off Poolewe untempting and we went instead to nearby Loch Thurnaig, where we found excellent shelter in a little cove at its south-west corner. A fisheries' research group keeps its boats there and we were invited to pick up one of their vacant moorings. We took the dinghy across the loch to a landing and got a lift from some members of the group into Poolewe, where we were to meet our daughter Alexa, her friend Dan Kiely, and Minna Guest, an old friend of ours. The return trip in the dinghy was wet and Minna, who had never sailed before, began to have misgivings about what was to come. However, a dinner of roast turkey put everyone in a good frame of mind, and the bright sunshine during the morning reinforced this happy mood. We cast off the mooring after lunch to make the most of the tidal streams and had a splendid reach up Loch Ewe with a SW Force 4. Once outside, the wind rose steadily to Force 6, and we approached Staffin Bay on Skye with a reef in the main. Staffin Bay, where we anchored in the late afternoon, is sheltered from the south-west. The wind continued to increase and when the 66ft. ketch *Sea Spirit*, belonging to Gordonstoun School, came in later, it was a solid Force 7 and *Sea Spirit* had shortened down to fore-staysail, trisail, and mizzen.

During the night, it was not only windy but also pouring with rain. We did not want to push our novices too fast and sailed to Portree on Thursday under only fore-staysail and reefed main, a snug combination. On Friday the wind abated and, after trying various directions, settled on the north-west as we proceeded to Mallaig past some fine scenery on Skye and the mainland opposite. *Sea Spirit* was already in Mallaig and we were invited to tie up to her. She had been purpose-built for the school in 1969 and had berths for a dozen students plus the skipper and a boatswain. Half the crew were girls, who ran the catering and seemed no less adept at working the ship than the boys.

Rain gave way to sunshine on Saturday, and we ran down to Tobermory under MPS in a mild north-westerly. By now Minna and Dan had settled down to our routine on *Quicksilver* and were enjoying themselves and being most useful. Alexa, who has sailed since the age of three months, was at once at home on *Quicksilver*. A walk around Tobermory in bright sunshine and a few jars in one of the hotels rounded off a pleasant day.

Sunday morning's mist and drizzle did not dampen our spirits and we set out down the Sound of Mull in a light northerly. After two hours the wind shifted to the west and hardened, and we roared through the Firth of Lorne and the Sound of Luing to Crinan at up to eight knots. Occasional flashes of sunlight illuminated the splendid landscape, which Germaine and I had last seen sixteen years before, after a transatlantic passage to Oban in *Minots Light*. Minna had her first turn at the wheel at speed, and it was hard to pry her loose when we arrived at the sea lock of the canal. We had been looking forward to one of the Crinan Hotel's renowned seafood dinners, but alas the hotel was closed while it was being rebuilt after a fire. After spending the night at the crowded basin in Crinan, we went through the canal on Monday. The rudeness and vile language of the lock-keepers came as a surprise; Germaine, Alexa and I are old hands at such trips and *Quicksilver* gave them no trouble. Perhaps they had the Monday morning blues. At 1600 we tied up in Ardrishaig and after a shopping expedition, had dinner at the Royal Hotel.

On Tuesday Minna had to return to London, and we missed the fresh outlook she had brought to our adventures. We motored in a calm via the Kyles of Bute to the Kip Marina. How fortunate are the sailors in western Scotland to have such glorious cruising grounds literally on their doorsteps. From Kip we went to Loch Ryan, where we anchored in Lady Bay. This is a good spot geographically from which to leave for Ireland, but the wash from the Belfast ferries rocked us all night and I will try to avoid the place next time. We took off early to make the most of the tidal streams and with the big reacher up and the Sailomat self-steerer doing the work, we had a peaceful sail in a wispy south-westerly to Strangford Lough in Northern Ireland. Chart 2156 of the Lough is one of the prettiest charts I have ever seen, a masterpiece of the cartographer's art, and the Lough matched its promise. We anchored in Audley's Roads under the ruined castle. Strangford comes from the Norse *strang fjord*, which means violent fjord, presumably because of the swift tidal streams in the narrows, and in fact we saw several yachts trying to sail against the stream and getting nowhere.

The tide necessitated an early start, and at 0540 we were speeding down the narrows past astonishing whirlpools. The wind was from the south-west at Force 5 and an ominous sky promised more, so we headed south under the conservative rig of fore-staysail and reefed main. As it happened, the wind never reached much further than Force 5 and we should have put up more sail, but *Quicksilver* was moving comfortably at six knots and we were content to let well alone. Late in the afternoon we reached Howth and were happy to be shown to a vacant mooring by the club's boatman.

A transatlantic race was being held in conunction with the ICC Cruise, and the larger yachts, *Kialoa, Ondine* and *Condor,* had just arrived when we reached Crosshaven. The size of these leviathans was brought home to us the next day when *Quicksilver* was at the Town Quay taking on fuel and *Condor*, nearly eighty feet of gleaming, varnished topsides, came alongside and asked to tie up to us. Not wishing to be the ham in such a sandwich, we left in a hurry. At the Royal Cork's marina we were happy to have a berth outside the US Naval Academy's sloop *Alliance* — even happier when Ian Morrison's *Querida* rafted outside us. However, we were progressively less pleased when six more yachts secured to *Querida* and a constant stream of people tramped across our decks at all hours. But the organization ashore was superb, and arrangements for laundry, for hiring a car and for repairing some sails were all carried out with a minimum of fuss.

Our stay at Crosshaven in the days before the cruise started was so pleasant that we could not quite see how the cruise could be better. In fact, as all the six or seven hundred participants can testify, the cruise was an immense success and especially rewarding to those who — like us — had never visited this splendid coast before. We left Crosshaven on Sunday, 22nd July, and had an exhilarating sail to Castlehaven in a SW Force 4/5 — our best sail of the year so far. *Quicksilver* loves going to windward and it was a treat to lower the centreboard and let her work up to weather of all challengers.

From Castlehaven we sailed in fog via Gascanane Sound and Long Island Bay to Crookhaven. Here *Keeshond*, with Gill and Peter Price and their sons, rafted to us and in the evening we joined another raft for a party that had as its theme the demolition of a keg of Guinness. A race around the Fastnet and on to Dunmanus Bay was proposed the next day for the larger yachts, but thick fog and a lack of wind caused this to be cancelled in favour of a parade to the Fastnet led by the radar-equipped *Deerhound*. At the lighthouse the fog cleared and several yachts landed dinghies there; we drifted while we ate lunch. Near Dunmanus Bay, a SW Force 3 came up, and we had a fine sail to Kitchen Cove under main and MPS.

Thursday saw us in Castletownbere where we anchored in the harbour for the CCA party at the local hotel. On Saturday we were host to a crowd of people — at one point fifteen were seated in the main cabin of *Quicksilver* — and in the evening we went in a hired local boat to the ICC festivities at Garnish Island. On Sunday Alexa and Dan left for Cork and, from there, home to California. It was a sad parting, but they certainly had had enough adventures to reflect upon until their next cruise with us. When they had gone, some of the crew members went to Garnish Island to see it in daylight while I checked

Suhaili on her return from her round-the-world voyage

PARAFFIN OIL COOKING STOVES.

(Special Oil Stove Catalogue sent on application.)

FIG. 1, 2 & 3.   FIG. 4.

FIG. 1.   SMALL DINNER STOVE, height $13\frac{3}{4}$ in., length 16 in., width $11\frac{1}{4}$ in
price, with utensils complete, **42s.**

FIG. 2.   MEDIUM DINNER STOVE, height $16\frac{1}{2}$ in., length 19 in., width $12\frac{1}{2}$ in
price, with utensils, **50s.** ; oval Boiler and Steamer, 8s. 6d. extra.

FIG. 3.   LARGE DINNER STOVE, height 17 in., length $20\frac{1}{2}$ in., width $14\frac{1}{4}$ in
price, with utensils, **55s.** ; oval Boiler and Steamer 8s. 6d. extra.

FIG. 4.   BREAKFAST STOVE, about, height $13\frac{3}{4}$ in., length $11\frac{1}{2}$ in., width $9\frac{1}{4}$ in
price **32s.** ; or of cheaper make, **25s,**

The Rippingville stove. In *The Riddle of the Sands* by Erskine Childers Davies telegrams Carruthers to bring out the No. 3 model

Vixen in the Solent, 1899

Dulcibella ex *Vixen*. Note the lifebo with the diagonal teak planking and remains of the counter, the deck be: still in place. Lymington 1942. *Pho Group Captain F.C. Griffiths RAF*

Colin McMullen, the skipper of *Saecwen*

Yeong showing her junk schooner rig

The Harrison Butler designed *Salamat* was built on the banks of the Bernam river by a Chinese man known as Mac

rideaux Haven,
esolation Sound. *Photo*
y Eric Hiscock

Harkaway

Pentina II in happier days

Quicksilver under spinnake
and with Arthur Beiser at t
helm.

St. Mary's Lifeboat during the 1979 Fastnet Race disaster

A rudderless crew await the arrival of a lifeboat

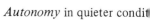
Autonomy in quieter conditi

Sarais Marais beating out to
the Needles

out the ship, a task I prefer to do alone on board. Unfortunately I did not have as company the babble that had been gushing forth from Channel 6 on the VHF during the cruise and which by now had almost all petered out; no longer would *Deerhound* treat us all to a spirited rendition of 'Lloyd George Knew My Father'.

The next phase of our summer plans called for a passage to the Mediterranean and the sunshine. *Quicksilver* reached Ile des Embiez, her Mediterranean base, on 1st September – the target date for arrival when we left Copenhagen at the end of May. This made the successful completion of the 4,000-mile cruise even more satisfying.

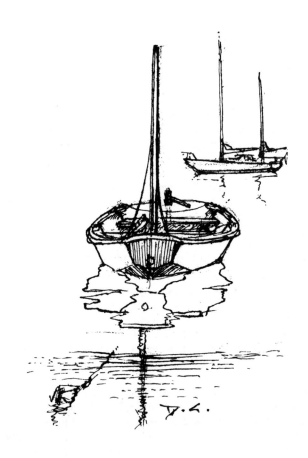

A short cruise in *Cheemaun* to a few of the Inland Waterways, Meers and Canals of Holland

by *Jack Bryans*

Cheemaun carries one 10ft. Souter sailing dinghy, one 10ft. Avon inflatable dinghy, one Mark 17 Kelvin Hughes Radar and a 'Pinta' automatic pilot.

After several visits to Rotterdam, Scheveningen, and Den Helder on passages to and from Finland, Sweden, and Denmark (one of which ended in a foul weather evasive passage from the Royal Maas Yacht Club to Flushing), the urge to revisit Holland grew until it became a must when we discussed it with the many friends we met on our return from Denmark in 1978. Accordingly, I set aside the whole of July 1979 for such a cruise, which should have given us nearly four weeks in those attractive waters, with two or three days at either end for the passage to and from the UK. However, it did not work out that way – for many reasons – and we had only sixteen days cruising in Dutch waters. Nevertheless, it provided a good initial experience for taking a 52ft. ship like *Cheemaun* with a 33ft. mast height through bridges, locks and canals. Although our cruise was disappointingly short, we gained much experience – especially as we were short-handed. We learned enough to want to go again at a more leisurely tempo with a crew of four or five.

Leaving Lymington in the afternoon of 6th July, Neville Burnett, Anne and I (average age seventy) picked up our mooring at Cowes for the night. The following morning we visited friends in Cowes, came back on board for lunch and soon afterwards were away in perfect weather to Brighton for the night. We spent twelve and a half hours in Brighton outside the lock, for which we were charged £9 – an exorbitant fee (£6.50 locked in last year). It was nearly three times any charge we had to meet in Holland, Belgium, or France for a full 24-hour stay.

At 0525 next day, 8th July, we sailed with a fair wind and tide, arriving at Ostend after fourteen hours at sea. We spent two nights at Ostend and moved on to Holland on the 10th, making an uneventful afternoon passage to Flushing, through the sea lock and on to Middleburg for the night. Customs were not available either at Flushing or Middleburg so we hauled down our Q flag. There is nothing to attract one to stay in Flushing, whereas Middleburg is a charming old place and a good shopping centre. There is a yacht basin, approached round

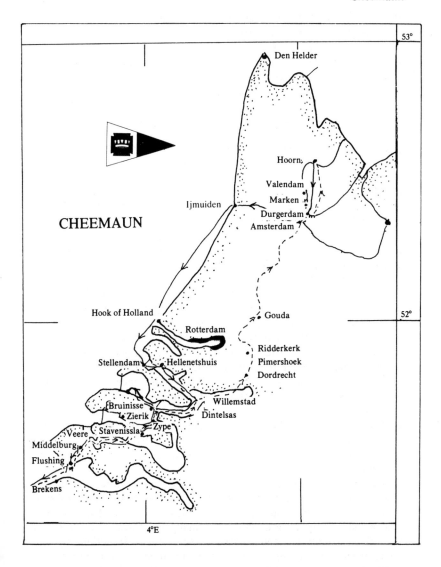

the north end of the town and entered through a bridge which opens frequently each day from 0830 onwards.

We anchored in the Sound on the far side of the long island opposite the town – Goudplaat Island. The southern end is a bird sanctuary and there is a special hard, with a minimum depth of about two metres, built so that boats can go alongside and watch. While we were in the Sound we scrubbed the decks and lowered both dinghies. We had a pleasant sail in the Penguin and there was a temptation to stay another night. We resisted the temptation and weighed at 1340, leaving the rubber dinghy inflated and upside down on the Penguin. As the day progressed, a stiff north-easterly produced quite a popple and spray on board, particularly after locking out at Zankreek. We had not planned a stop for the night; we had a quiet look at Bruinissi but eventually reached the special lock for yachts at Oost Helligat.

At Willemstad we secured alongside a Dutch yacht, *Renee*, whose owner was a close friend of Aylett Moore. There were cows grazing just thirty feet away from us and a wide variety of birds, with their young, swam round us. Unfortunately it started to rain – for the first time since we left Lymington – and it persisted all day; we had to don oilskins when we went shopping. Nevertheless, we enjoyed Willemstad and would like to return on a sunnier day. No wonder we had bad luck with the weather: it was Friday the 13th after all.

We left at 1600 and took the Oude Maars to Dordrecht where we secured at 1845 in a little cut just north of the Cathedral. We had had to wait some time for the railway bridge to open. Bridges and locks, apart from sea locks do not open at weekends. Once they are closed for the weekend, you have to stay where you are.

Apart from incessant ringing of the Cathedral bell, Dordrecht is a pleasant town, with a good market and at least one interesting museum, which we discovered near where we berthed. Charlotte van Smirna, from the Dutch Red Cross, visited by car from Den Haag on the Sunday.

We had been advised to get to the bridge leading to Rotterdam and just north of Dordrecht before 0700 to avoid the early morning rush hour, so we planned an early start, only to be told that our little bridge did not open until 0800. We finally got through at 0936 and started on a fateful inland passage to Amsterdam, something we will never again attempt with masts. All the same it was a useful experience. With only three of us on board it was quite impossible to keep a detailed log; it was just a succession of slow down, wait, follow through at every bridge and the bridges were interminable. So many boats were going the same way that some gave up and turned back, but others joined us as we arrived at connecting canals along the route. Of course, the answer is to do this cruise in late May and June, not at the height of the holiday season, and preferably without masts.

A collection of some twenty boats eventually arrived at the motorway bridge and lock to the south of Amsterdam. The time this was due to open changed several times after the arrival of a barge whose skipper had overslept and failed to advise of his late arrival. He, of course, had priority but before he led the way in, he rammed and damaged a small yacht, which caused even longer delay. This was an inefficient performance for the Dutch and a frustrating one for the yachts' tired crews. We eventually locked in and made the fascinating night passage through the centre of Amsterdam, waiting at every bridge. We finally arrived at that famous railway bridge which only opens once a day – at 0200. We got through at about 0245, 17th July, and decided to go on through the last road bridge before the Nord Zee Canal. We found a perfect berth waiting for us just outside on the port hand, where we secured at 0330. Then it was Bovril and bed: we had been on the move for nearly twenty hours.

The morning of the 17th was spent in Amsterdam, doing some shopping and sight-seeing. I bought the two Dutch charts covering Den Helder to Flushing. I had decided to return south again via Ijmuiden and the open sea to the Hook. In the afternoon we had sufficiently recovered from the previous night's ordeal. After lunch we made for the Ijsselmeer which is reached via a road bridge and a lock. The lock is a ghastly affair with projecting buttresses all along it making it impossible to lie comfortably alongside. Damage to a boat like *Cheemaun*, with her forward flare and teak guard-rail and bulwarks is almost inevitable. However, after much fendering and cursing we got through with only minor scrapes and were out of the Nord Zee Canal and into the Ijsselmeer (formerly the Zuider Zee). The channel followed by barges is buoyed for a mile or so but there appears to be an overall minimum depth of about two and a half metres; after the second buoy, we set a course to clear the lighthouse off Marken and thence for Hoorn, which I was determined to visit. We decided to anchor for the night in the open water just inside the breakwater, where it is fairly sheltered and shallow. Two other yachts were there. The wind was westerly 3/4.

At 0200 on the 18th I was awakened by the rustling of trees in the wind. I went on deck and found our stern right up against the shore and the said trees almost overhead. I woke the crew by starting both engines. We got the anchor up and put it down again in the same place as before in eight feet of water and for good measure veered to ten fathoms, after which we must only have been riding to the chain. Subsequently, when we weighed, a length of leather was jammed between the shank and flukes and this probably stopped the anchor from digging in. I just do not know: five fathoms of chain in eight feet of water ought to be enough for any boat in a Force 3/4 breeze.

We put the rubber dinghy over the side the following morning and Neville and I took it into the inner harbour to prospect. It rained; but there was good shopping and a market day in full swing, with bands playing and all sorts of stalls. We fixed to buy some fuel and I visited the harbour-master at the marine, who gave me a berth for two nights on the end of one of their long pontoons.

From our friend Yvonne Reints, whom we met here, we learned that there is a sea lock just north of Goeree, leading into Haringvleit and situated just north of Stellendam. This would save having to go all the way up to Rotterdam against a foul tide and take us straight back to the attractive meer area.

We spent two nights at Hoorn and had one of our two meals ashore during the cruise at a little pub by the quayside: delicious beer and sandwiches. High winds persisted but we could stay no longer; we cast off and retraced our route to that ghastly lock and then back into the Nord Zee Kanal. Yvonne had told us of Sixhaven, a quiet little marina on the north side of the canal and opposite the station. We just managed to squeeze into a berth on the port hand by the entrance.

An interesting feature of the passage from Hoorn was that we were closely followed by hundreds of terns. I can only think that our speed over the shallow water disturbed the bottom so that something of interest to the birds was brought to the surface.

High winds and heavy showers persisted and the forecast in the North Sea was 6/7, so we stayed a second night. Really heavy hail and thunder hit us at about tea-time, then the weather started to improve and only Force 5 from the north-west was forecast in the North Sea.

There is a pleasant canal just west of Sixhaven and an attractive pool and village about a mile and a half up. We were also close by the ferry to Amsterdam and the Shell building towered above us to the west. Sixhaven is an excellent marina and ideal for a short stay in Amsterdam, away from the noise and traffic yet within easy reach of everything by ferry.

We left the marina at 0720 on 22nd July and headed for Ijmuiden. The railway bridge opened for us and with a fine day and only showers to the north of us, we locked in at Ijmuiden at 0940. Two other boats were also bound for the same lock as ourselves, but they got no further than the breakwater before they turned back. They missed a lovely sail.

I set a course to clear the Hook and we rolled our way southwards with a Force 5 a point abaft the beam. *George* (the Pinta) steered very well, which was fortunate – in that sea and wind, hand-steering would have been very tiring. By 1430 we were a half mile off the entrance to Europort; from there we steered along the line of buoys off the shallow waters north of Goeree. It was here that chart no. 1447 would have helped us because our coastal chart gave very few soundings; we saw several marks which, no doubt, would have been shown on no. 1447 but were not shown on ours. However, I had taken the precaution of time our arrival within an hour of HW Hook, so there was little to fear. I subsequently cut the corner a bit and never had less than fifteen feet all the way in. We picked up the buoyed channel and from then on it was easy. A lovely sunny evening greeted us as we entered Haringvleit.

Hellevortsluis, a charming town at the north end of this meer, was only three miles away and we found a convenient berth in the marina to the westward. (Anchoring is prohibited off the harbour.) An alternative berth would have been up the canal which passes through the centre of the town. Boats secured there looked lovely in the evening sunshine and I half wished I had taken *Cheemaun* there. Our berth was some way from the town but was worth the walk to see Hellevortsluis.

We left at 1130 Monday, 23rd July, and had an uneventful passage to the Heringvleutborg, the bridge leading to the Nordhollandsch Deip and Dordrecht. This opened fairly quickly and we anchored for lunch in the more northern of the two little bays on the starboard hand by the Zuider Voorhaven lock. We locked in at 1530, one of thirty-three yachts going west; forty-nine came through, going east. This explains why the authorities decided on a special lock for yachts.

Here, in Volkerak and later Krammer, the waters are tidal. We started to retrace our outward passage to Dordrecht. I had my eye on Grevelingen Meer, about which our friend in Ostend had told us. At 1755 we locked in at Bruinisse, where we were in non-tidal waters again. We took the north-west passage, Grevelingen, as far as the island of Stampersplaat and then turned westward and finally secured for the night to a jetty north of the lock gates leading to Brouwershaven. This was an attractive passage in the evening sunlight and it was only a short walk into the town. The harbour master offered to keep the lock gates open for us on our arrival but we were obviously better off outside; inside it was very crowded.

One could easily spend a week in this meer, anchoring at carefully chosen spots, sailing the dinghy and generally relaxing. Unfortunately, lack of time made this impossible for us. Returning to Bruinisse, we locked out into tidal waters again and passed through that uninteresting Mastgat and Keeten leading to the Zeelandbrug just south of Zierikzee and on south to the lock at the east end of Noord Beveland. Just off the lead into this lock I distinguished myself by anchoring for lunch with ten fathoms of cable in twelve fathoms of water. There seems to be a bit of a rise and fall there but I never checked. We locked in and out and ended an eventful day at anchor close to the bird sanctuary at the south end of Haringvreter Island, off Verre, and on the west side of the channel as the wind was blowing westerly (easterly on our outward passage). Yachts passed us heading south; the locals are so unaccustomed to the idea of anchoring that one actually asked us if we had engine trouble!

We stopped at Verre for some fuel and a quick run round that charming place, which Neville had not seen before. We then went on to Middleburg for our last night in Holland. I had decided that Middleburg is so close to Flushing that there is no point in going that short distance before departing for Belgium or France and home. In the event, we left Flushing at 1010, having decided to spend a night at Dunkirk. From there we had a foggy run back to Lymington via Brighton marina.

NOTES

1   *Crew*
    A total of only three on board is not enough for a cruise like this with a boat as large as *Cheemaun*. Four is a minimum. A larger crew would have meant far less strain, particularly at bridges and locks.

2   *Date*
    July is not the time to go. The end of May or June would be better, before the height of the holiday season.

3   *Rig*
    Masts are a distinct disadvantage, other than for hoisting dinghies in and out. A completely different route could have been taken to reach Hoorn and the one we did take could have been easier.

4   *Hull*
    Cheemaun's hull, with her forward flare and high wooden bulwarks and guard-rail, is very vulnerable in locks. We were lucky not to sustain some more serious damage – thanks to the splendid routine which Anne and Neville adopted. One more crew was needed. Dutch locks are designed for barges!

5   *Charts*
    There are two excellent publications: the *ANWB Waterkaart* and the *Kaart Voor Ziel-en Motoyachten*. Both are published annually. One thing, however, must be carefully watched, and that is the scale. This will change not only from *kaart* to *kaart* but sometimes from page to page within one *kaart* issue. Scales range from 1:25,000 to 1:100,000. Inset plans of some major towns are provided.

6   *Publications*
    The above mentioned charts and *Inland waterways of the Netherlands*, in three volumes by E.E. Benest, Imray, Laurie, Norie & Wilson are essential.

7   *Passages to and from*
    Going east, the north coasts of France and Belgium are best – if only because you can carry a fair tide for most of the way. Going west, however, I am not sure it is not better to do a night passage and cross the shipping lanes before the straits of Dover. Crossing the shipping lanes going west makes the tidal problem almost impossible from the French coast.

PALAFOX 2, THROUGH THE EYE OF A NEEDLE:
A Cruise to South Brittany through the Ille and Rance Canals
by Pam Senior

Harry and I had our first introduction to cruising in 1966, when we crewed for a friend to the Baie de Douarnenez and back to Fowey in a Nicholson 32. On this trip we learned exactly what cruising was about, and it inspired us to want a boat of our own. We loved the Nicholson but felt that as we were beginners and had started rather late in life, it was not the yacht for us. Instead we decided to order a 30ft. Seadog GRP ketch, *Palafox*; it reduced sail easily and had a more powerful engine than the Nicholson. It was delivered in May 1967. Shortly afterwards I underwent a major operation but had recovered sufficiently to take part in a cruise to the Channel Islands and northern France. Our son and a friend of his accompanied us on this trip and everything went splendidly.

Then we cruised the coast of South Brittany more extensively, always with one or other of our two sons. After that we managed on our own and came to enjoy complete independence and the pleasure of our own company.

The winter of 1979, however, was the beginning of the end for us both. I had arthritis in one hip, and Harry, who had passed his seventieth birthday, had it in his hips and spine and was unable to bend. We realised that we would have to sell *Palafox* at the end of the season but we were determined to have a final, special cruise. Our problems would include mooring, anchoring, and dinghy work, although once on board we could manage the boat adequately, particularly with the help of our roller-reefing headsail, which enabled us to avoid foredeck work in heavy weather.

We decided to sail to St. Malo, through the Ille and Rance canals, via Rennes into the Vilaine river, and out into the sea from La Roche Bernard. This trip would involve taking out masts, so we had some crutches made to fit the two tabernacles for the masts and rigging to lie along. The Brittany canal system is 160-miles long with sixty-three locks; we knew we could not manage the locks without extra help. We also felt unable to cope with the dismasting by ourselves; although I, with typical optimism, visualized a helpful yard at either end to do everything for us.

By this time we found that a friend, Frank, of about our own age and quite inexperienced in sailing, was keen to join us – and particularly enthusiastic about taking out and replacing the masts.

Palafox II

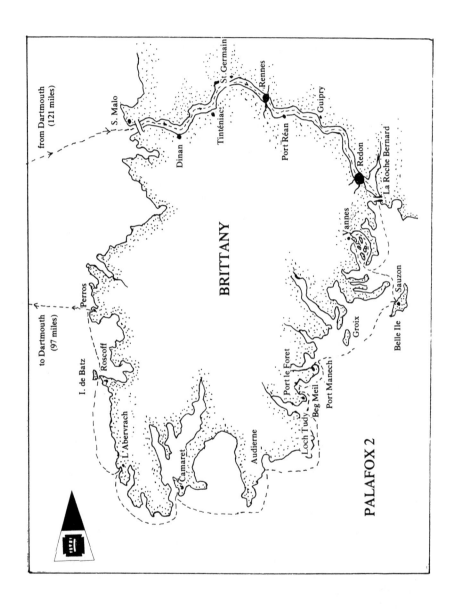

88

We stowed ship on Sunday, 17th June and spent the night on our mooring, ready to set off early next morning. The forecast was for light and variable winds and we had to motor-sail for several hours. Later we were able to switch off and we sailed with ease all the way to St. Malo. On the way we saw two schools of porpoises in the sea and two Concorde jets in the sky. It was lovely passing Guernsey and Jersey and having the lights of Les Hanois, Roche Douvres and La Corbière to guide us. We tied up to a buoy off Dinard on Tuesday at 1430; we enjoyed a cup of coffee and congratulated ourselves on managing to sail so much of the way and having saved fuel. We set off again and were soon through the barrage into the Rance and anchored for the night opposite St. Suliac.

On Wednesday we started up the Rance and went through the first lock in such low water that the channel marker posts were out on the mud. We had no idea at the time when the water was let in or out of the barrage and we continued to the Chatelier lock in practically no water at all. The lock-keeper saw us coming and waved us back with horrified gestures, telling us to return at 1600. We turned downstream, tied to a convenient buoy and took the ground at a great list. The tide was let in a little later and we floated once more. However, the water-level dropped again almost immediately, but then it started to rise, at first slowly and then with such a huge surge that we broke away from the buoy. I actually heard the water coming up – just like the Severn Bore.

We passed through the lock out of the Rance Maritime and on to Dinan, where we tied up at the fuel quay. Unfortunately, we were told that we could not refuel, not because of a lack of diesel but because the tanker had put diesel in the petrol tank and vice versa and both tanks had to be cleaned out. Luckily we had only used seven gallons.

We then set to work taking the masts out; Frank went up the mizen to disconnect the triatic stay so that we could lift the mizen-mast out with the main halyard. We worked until midnight – with only a short dinner break – until we had sails, booms, shrouds removed and stowed and there was nothing left to do except lift out the main-mast with the crane the following morning. Frank was enthusiastic and indefatigable throughout, but Harry and I were wondering whether we would be able to put it all together again.

The next morning the harbour-master arrived at 0800 with the key to the crane and we soon had the main-mast on the quay. The harbour-master grumbled throughout our operation; luckily Harry did not understand that he was telling us we were mad to try to get a boat that size through to the Vilaine and compared it to a camel passing through the eye of a needle.

After this brief tirade we dealt with the fantastic tangle of shrouds, halyards, topping lifts, stays, booms, crosstrees, and a radar reflector, and eventually made them into a neat bundle — with the RCC burgee stuck in the middle — which we lashed together to lie along the crutches. At 1530 we decided to sail under the bridge and out of Dinan and found ourselves in a narrow, green tunnel, overhung with trees. We began wondering what we had let ourselves in for but we soon came to some beautiful scenery. We passed through seven locks very easily, with the help of some pleasant lock-keepers. We moored at Evran for the night and dined peacefully on board *Palafox*.

On Friday the 22nd, we left Evran and sailed through about eight locks before nosing into the bank for lunch. The locks are charming, each one a little farm with animals and poultry scurrying about. All the lock-keepers were amazed at the size of our boat, particularly as so few go through at that time of the year. That night we moored to the quay at Tinteniac, where there was an almost uninhabited caravan site. There we were able to have hot showers and then enjoy our first French meal at an attractive hotel. *Palafox* looked so neat; we were totally unencumbered by masts and rigging and could use the cockpit hood in the normal way.

We left at 0930 on Saturday and during the day went through twenty-one locks, including the *escalier* of eleven locks, which brought us to the summit of the canal. The water was very shallow and we squelched through the mud, wondering what would happen if we got stuck with no one to pull us off. Descending the locks, however, was much easier and far less tiring than ascending — especially as we had become proficient in the drill.

We reached St. Germain at 1830 and tied up for the night at the pretty little quay. The weather, which had been hot and sunny, was now beginning to cool. When we awoke on Sunday the 24th, it was raining. We got up late and had lunch just below the lock. There was a splendid morning market in full swing; the lock-keeper was there, enjoying himself immensely, so we had to work the lock ourselves.

After lunch we were delayed at St. Gregoire lock, where a mass of spectators were watching a procession of boats containing people in fancy dress, part of a water carnival. We were unable to pull into the side as there was not enough water, so we slowly motored on to Rennes, where we had to negotiate a tangle of canal, river and road bridges. At last we tied up at a quay in the Vilaine river, alongside the road and opposite a fuel station. We dined and then slept soundly.

In the morning I did some shopping and then we took on sixty litres of diesel after three trips with the jerry can. One of the lock-keepers had warned us that the water-level would be rather low, so I telephoned the Vilaine water authority to make sure we would be all right. After their reassurances, we set off at mid-morning. The first lock we encountered incorporated a swing bridge, where we had to wait for several barges. A man watching from the bank was amazed that we had come from St. Malo. '*Pas possible*,' he said.

At lunch-time we reached Pont Rean, an attractive riverside town rather similar to Lechlade-on-Thames. We had some lunch and a siesta and then made a satisfactory trip to the market. We also checked our fuel and were encouraged to find that we had only used fifteen gallons since we left Dartmouth. We made an earlier start than usual from Pont Rean as we wanted to reach Guipry by the evening. We were now quite confident and thought we knew all about locks; furthermore the Vilaine had widened. The lock at La Boel was particularly beautiful, and we passed through it in a state of euphoria. After rounding a corner we passed a sign on the starboard side; we had no idea what it meant and, to our dismay, we were soon hard aground, with a small French yacht also aground just ahead of us. There were some black plastic cans, intended as marker buoys, which we had passed to starboard instead of port; in the middle of the river in front of us was a huge pile of stones. Everything had happened so quickly; we were in real difficulty for the first time on our journey.

The French people on the yacht could not help us and we could not help them. However, the Frenchman got into his dinghy and somehow managed to pull the yacht towards the bank; after half an hour they were away. We tried to follow their example; we took the dinghy ashore and wound a line round a tree to winch ourselves forward; to no avail. Finally, Harry realised that we should try to get back the way we had come. He and Frank took the kedge upstream in the dinghy and at last we moved slowly back, then round the first marker buoy and off along the river. The bottom of the Ille and Rance canal is soft, but that of the Vilaine is hard. We had had a nasty hour and a half.

We continued our journey very carefully, and I was below preparing lunch, when we hit another obstruction in mid-stream. This gave us a fright but did not impede our progress. We eventually tied up just short of Le Galière lock, all of us rather shaken after our experiences. We passed several smaller warning signs later on and paid great heed to them; but even so we twice hit hidden hazards in mid-stream. All in all it was a nerve-racking day.

We passed through the lock at Guipry and at 1645 tied up at Station Verte; we were exhausted. Harry and I did a lot of cleaning before drinks-time, and as the hotel was not very enticing, we dined on board.

We left Guipry early on Wednesday the 27th. We had another unscheduled bump before the last lock and later passed some warning areas — without any trouble. The final lock, at Melon, took us into the Vilaine Maritime and the water steadily increased in depth. We began to relax.

We reached Beste at 1130 — too early for lunch, which we ate later at a charming restaurant in La Chapelle St. Melaine. We would have liked to have spent the night at La Chapelle St. Melaine, but instead we carried on to Redon where we planned to replace the masts. We stopped in the main stream of the town but then later went under a bridge through an open lock, and into the *bassin*. We tied to a finger pontoon and arranged to get the key to the crane at 1030 the next morning. We were a long way from the town, so we went shopping and then dined on board.

It was very hot the following morning, but we soon had the boat under the crane at the far end of the basin, where we began to lay out everything on the quayside in preparation for our task. At 1030 I rowed across to get the key from the little Chef du Port; when I returned we got down to business. A young Frenchman, who was painting his boat nearby, came over to give us a hand with the crane; we all worked hard in the fierce heat until noon. After lunch we attended to the mizen and at least twenty-nine shrouds, stays, halyards and so on. We tightened the bottle-screws too much at first and had to remove all the split pins and start again. Frank enjoyed himself, even when he had to go up the mizen-mast twice to adjust twisted shrouds and free the main halyard. We had almost finished with the sails and roller-reefing gear when we were asked to move to make way for another yacht.

As we motored away we noticed that the lock entrance was blocked by ropes and posts and a sign saying '*Danger*'. Our French neighbours told us that all the workers at a factory nearby had been sacked and in protest had tipped an articulated lorry trailer into the canal and blocked the entrance. The next morning, however, by keeping well to starboard and proceeding very carefully, we managed to get out.

From here on, the river is wide and deep. We quickly passed through the large swing bridge and arrived at Folieux for lunch. (Folieux is a pleasant little yachting port on the starboard hand and not far from Beganne.) We felt more confident now that the yacht was properly rigged. We were only an hour from La Roche Bernard and after passing under the big new bridge, we tied up at the new marina, alongside a local Dartmouth yacht, *Yanuca*. However, we were moved round the great rock to the old port, where we took on diesel from the quayside and then moved to a pontoon. We had now reached the furthest point of our cruise and decided to stay for two nights to give us time to explore.

We left at 0900 on Sunday, 1st July, and sailed through the barrage with about a dozen other yachts. We then put up all sail and, with a lovely NW Force 3/4, had a superb sail to the Golfe du Morbihan. Everything was working splendidly and we had a wonderful time; we even saw a school of porpoises, which increased our enjoyment.

We arrived at the entrance to the Golfe with a foul tide; we hove-to, had tea and then motor-tacked as far as Ile Berder to anchor just south-west of the moorings.

The following morning was hot, sunny and windless, so we motored slowly up to Vannes and tied up on a pontoon close to that of the harbour-master. Vannes is a lovely place now that there is a marina there instead of dreadful mud.

On Tuesday we could not leave until the canal bridge opened at 1130. Instead we occupied ourselves with cleaning and shopping and after lunch we had a wonderful sail round the outer islands on the east side and up along the Ile aux Moines to anchor off our favourite beach. We enjoyed a late lunch and a siesta in hot sunshine and little wind and with the Golfe looking its best. I had a swim round the boat and Harry and Frank rowed ashore to explore the village.

The next day we rose early, only to find that our anchor chain was entangled with a lobster pot. Nevertheless, we set off for the open sea after only a short delay. We motor-sailed to Sauzon, Belle Ile, where we anchored in the inner harbour and enjoyed a cup of coffee. We had a cooling swim, after which the tide began to fall. As soon as we took the ground, we began cleaning the hull to remove all the oil and dirt that we had picked up in the canals. We also inspected for possible damage. Apart from some weed round the impeller, all was well, so we scrubbed away until the sun was over the yard-arm. Then we sat back to enjoy one of our favourite anchorages.

We weighed anchor at 1015 on Thursday, 5th July. There was promise of wind but this soon died and we had a slow sail towards Concarneau, leaving Ile de Groix to starboard. We saw several sharks and five French mine-sweepers towing enormous trawls. At 1630 a good wind blew up and we had a fine sail into the Aven river, anchoring off Port Manech at 1930. On the way, we had caught several mackerel, which Harry filleted for supper. I rounded off the evening with a swim in the quiet darkness.

We had a peaceful night and left Port Manech at 1030 with little wind but in brilliant sunshine. After mid-day we had a delightful sail and anchored for lunch at 1330 just north of Begmeil. We rowed ashore after our siesta and had a super warm bathe in the shallow water. We then motored the short distance to the marina at Baie de la Forêt, where we tied up, showered and had a delicious meal at a little café near the port. It was the hottest day we had encountered so far.

On Saturday, Harry and Frank walked up to do the weekend shopping while I cleaned up. We refuelled before leaving for a gentle sail along the coast and later anchored for lunch off the south beach of Ile Tudy, where we had another swim before entering the harbour to take a buoy. In the harbour we saw RCC *Respect* and Harry rowed over to visit the Cresswells, who were on their way home after a two-month cruise.

The following morning it was cold and grey and we made our way north to Audierne in bad visibility. There was very little wind to round Penmarch, but we had a fine sail to anchor in St. Evette in company with several English yachts. I had my last swim in very cold water.

We left at 0830 the next morning so that we would catch the tide through the Raz. There was very little wind, but it improved later and we enjoyed a gentle sail towards Camaret. The cold weather demanded that our routine gin and lime should be replaced by hot soup. We were able to use our mizen staysail (for the first time on the cruise) until we went through the Passage des Toulinguets and into Camaret. On the pontoon we met *Gilda*, a local yacht, and had drinks with the Dowells. We used the dinghy to go shopping to avoid the long walk into town. The French police told us that yachts are no longer allowed to anchor out in the harbour and were busy moving one such vessel out.

We left on the morning of the 10th under full sail; unfortunately it was another cold, grey day and the wind soon dropped. Harry let me pilot our boat into Le Conquêt and after lunch, we returned to the Chenal du Four, where we beat up in rather rough water but with the benefit of a few rays of sun. There was a big swell as we rounded the Four lighthouse and it remained fairly rough until we had passed Le Libenter. We took a buoy at L'Abervrach, close to RCC *Balkis*, a beautiful Excalibur. We were invited on board by the Norris's and their family and then had supper in our own cockpit.

The next morning, after an early lunch, we left via the Malouine Passage, close-hauled after that and then enjoyed a good free wind for two hours. We then suffered poor visibility and had difficulty sighting the lighthouse on the Ile de Batz. We finally dropped anchor just inside the harbour of Porz Kernoch at 1900. It was so peaceful and as we gently took the ground for the night, the sunset was stunning.

On Thursday, we had to leave by 1130 on a falling and foul tide going east; we anchored in the ferryport to wait for the tide. We waved to Dru Bethel in RCC *Acquest* before leaving for a slow passage to Perros. We locked in at 2015 in time to see RCC *La Snook* and two other yachts, but we were too far away to make contact with them.

On Friday the 13th, we prepared for our Channel crossing, feeling sad that we were leaving France for the last time in *Palafox*. We left at 1015 with a NW Force 4 but at 1700 we ran into dense fog; at the same time a large French schooner ghosted past us. We heard two ships' hooters very close to us and donned our life-jackets, then a tanker passed uncomfortably close to our bows. Luckily the fog cleared by 1845 and we had a good – but cold – sail towards Start Point, across the bay and into Dartmouth. We reached our mooring at 1045.

Our last cruise in *Palafox* had been interesting and successful; we had never had more than a drop of rain and our sprayhood had been unused. We had never been held up and the engine had worked perfectly throughout. On the whole it had been an easy cruise – the hardest part being dropping and raising the masts. I could hardly walk when we finally came ashore with all our gear; but we had accomplished what we had set out to do.

Palafox was put on the market at once; there were no immediate takers, so we decided to come up to the RCC Beaulieu meet and leave her at Lymington. Our final sail was a brisk, sparkling trip to Lymington from Beaulieu. We spent a night on board and then worked hard to get *Palafox* ship-shape.

My worst moment was when I locked the cabin door for the last time, before we were driven to the bus stop to start our journey home. I confess that I wept.

			Log	Hours	Mooring	Fee	Engine Hours
June							
Sun	17	Dartmouth	121	33	anchor	–	3
Mon	18	At sea			alongside quay	8fr.	all engine
Tue	19	S. Suliac (opp.)			moor	–	all engine
Wed	20	Dinan			moor	–	all engine
Thur	21	Evran			moor	–	all engine
Fri	22	Tenténiac			moor	–	all engine
Sat	23	St. Germain			moor	–	all engine
Sun	24	Rennes	73	6 days	moor	–	all engine
Mon	25	Pont Rean			moor	–	all engine
Tue	26	Guipry			moor	–	all engine
Wed	27 Thur 28	Redon	58	3 days	marina	–	all engine
Fri	29 Sat 30	La Roche Bernard	26	4½ days	marina	38.50fr.	all engine
July							
Sun	1	Ile Berder, Morbihan	31	9	anchor	–	½
Mon	2	Vannes, Morbihan	7	2	marina	5fr.	1
Tue	3	Ile aux Moines	15	3½	anchor	–	2
Wed	4	Sauzon, Belle Ile	24	5½	anchor	–	2
Thur	5	Port Manech	41	9½	anchor	–	3
Fri	6	Port le Forêt	16	4	marina	39fr.	1
Sat	7	Loch Tudy	17	4	buoy	20fr.	2
Sun	8	Audierne	28	7½	anchor	–	3
Mon	9	Camaret	29	6½	marina	25fr.	2
Tue	10	L'Abervrach	30	7½	buoy	27fr.	2
Wed	11	Porz Kernoch, Ile de Batz	31	5½	anchor	–	1
Thur	12	Perros	29	5½	marina	19.30fr.	2
Fri	13	At sea	1		–	–	–
Sat	14	Dartmouth	97	24	own buoy		2
		TOTAL TRIP	674				

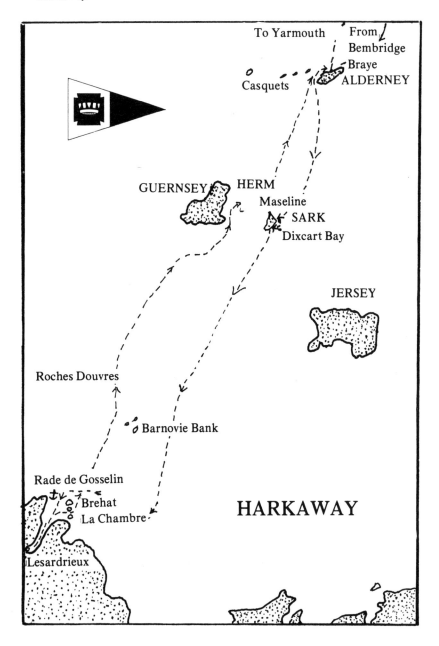

CRUISE TO THE CHANNEL ISLANDS AND BRITTANY

by *Andrew J.S. O'Grady*

We bought *Harkaway* in the spring of 1978. We knew that she was not an ideal cruising boat, but we decided that she was better than nothing at all. *Harkaway* is a 21ft. yacht (alternatively, a 16ft. yacht with a 5ft. overhang) and with a 5ft. beam. She was built of pitch pine on oak in 1947 by Alan Pape of Looe. My wife Sally and I spent a year rejuvenating her: she was stripped to bare wood, in and out; rotten wood, including deck beams and floors, was replaced; new keel bolts were put in, and a multitude of other alterations and additions were made. Contrary to all our expectations, the internal stripping was by far the most difficult the time-consuming task. By Easter 1979 *Harkaway* was ready to be launched. The vessel was lifted on to a trailer using a hydraulic jack and then towed from my father's garden to the sea.

On 12th April we launched *Harkaway* at Bembridge Harbour. As we expected she soon started to leak. 'Don't worry, she'll soon take up,' we were told repeatedly. After ten weeks we still could not leave her for more than a couple of days without fear of her sinking. (All credit goes to the boatman who regularly pumped her out for us.) Consequently, a week's holiday was spent refastening and recaulking the garboard strake. After that there were no more problems and we had many happy, wet weekends sailing on the Solent. At last we had the confidence in *Harkaway* to be able to start planning a summer cruise. Our aim was to make Mont St. Michel.

Saturday, 18th August 1979 We set sail from Bembridge for Alderney. It was difficult to decide when to leave as the forecast was NW 5, locally 6, and it was only five days since the Fastnet tragedy. However, we were assured by the Southampton weatherman that it would not worsen, so off we went. We reached St. Catherine's Point by lunchtime, having sped along a smooth sea with a twenty-knot off-shore wind. Under these conditions it was necessary to have two reefs in the mainsail and to set the storm jib — which may give some idea of how tender *Harkaway* is. We always have to reduce sail early.

We were greeted by a confused sea at St. Catherine's. However, the wind moderated in the afternoon and gave us a pleasant reach towards Alderney. It was pleasing to find the lights of Cap de la Hague at 2200 — just when we expected. We had no log so it was difficult to estimate speed. We altered course to avoid being swept into the

Harkaway

Race and arrived in Braye Harbour on the darkest night either of us had ever experienced.

Sunday, 19th August We remained on Alderney for the day, scrubbed the bottom of *Harkaway*, had tea with the Campbells (RCC) on *Rosalind* and gazed longingly at the mass of – sadly – not quite ripe blackberries. On our return to Alderney we managed to pick enough for one meal.

Monday, 20th August Regrettably, the forecast was still for strong north-westerly winds and the general synopsis spoke of several approaching lows. There were only four days before the top of spring tides, so it became clear that my longed-for trip to Mont St. Michel was not possible. Rather sadly we sailed for Sark instead.

We were encouraged to sail close inshore by Malcolm Robson's Channel Island Pilot. This was very exciting but we had difficulty finding one of the transits he gave, despite an intensive search. I think this may be because *Harkaway* has very little freeboard, the tide was low at the time, and we were suffering from lack of height. However, weaving among the rocks was certainly a highlight of our holiday. On reaching Maseline, Sark, we found difficulty getting into the anchorage; there were large areas of calm in the lee of the cliffs and the currents were sweeping us towards the rocky lighthouse promontory. In a frenzy of activity I struggled to fix the outboard motor in position, while Sally continued trying to sail into the bay. As usual in such circumstances, we had passed the danger under sail by the time the motor was ready to start.

We found it was delightful to wander round Sark – once we had conquered the steep hill up to the village. The complete lack of motor vehicles enhanced its appeal by enabling one to wander along the centre of the streets without fear for one's life.

Sally and I celebrated our second wedding anniversary here. It was a beautiful sunny day, just as we had hoped, but it soon became apparent that Sark didn't cater for rather tatty sailors such as us; so we cooked a special meal on our primus and indulged ourselves with our newly acquired stocks of duty free liquor. Later that evening we were invited aboard Sir Thomas Lee's (RCC) boat *Cardhu* and spent a jolly time with him and his splendid crew of nine. They persuaded us to swim with them early the next morning, a feat for which we were well rewarded with a cooked breakfast – an unheard of treat on *Harkaway*. After some crew swapping, Tom found himself on his way to Dixcart Bay with an entirely female crew of eight and *Harkaway* was hot on the trail. Dixcart Bay was a lovely spot, surrounded by beautiful woodland and coastal walks. However, the swell was relentless, as – we were beginning to realise – were the anchoring habits of our 'Cross-Channel Comrades'.

Wednesday, 22nd August The wind was now in the west, so we set off to beat down to the Pontrieux River. It was a long, hard day: we missed the tide at our destination and had a long beat up to the entrance. Entering the Grand Channel, we struggled for hours against the tide, which was running at least three knots. We were making no progress, so we eventually resorted to the outboard and motored a mile to the nearest anchorage in Rade de Pommelin. It took us an hour and a half to cover that last mile.

Everything was soaked. *Harkaway* with her notional freeboard is a very wet and uncomfortable boat, so Sally had a lot to put up with that day. Sally is as good a sailing companion as one could wish for, but I made the mistake of introducing her to cruising on a large and comfortable yacht — the type that only gets wet when it rains. *Harkaway* was something of a change.

Thursday, 23rd August The morning found us in an anchorage far from land and very exposed to the SW 6/7 that was blowing in. The anchor was holding well but we preferred to seek shelter under Ile de Bréhat. I put two reefs in the main and hauled away. All hell was let loose as the sail flogged violently. Suddenly, the luff groove split along half its length on the port side, thus freeing the sail from the mast. Down came the sail and with it all hope of beating up to shelter. It was obvious I would have to effect a repair. I did not think I could climb the mast in those conditions and besides I had foolishly forgotten to stow any glue. The only solution was to motor up to Lezardrieux where we could buy the missing supplies. It was heart-breaking to shame the Club burgee by motoring up the river as other boats stormed by under sail. We had quite a struggle under power. Waves repeatedly swamped the air intake and stopped the engine. Luckily, it always started again at first pull, just in time to save us from drifting on to the jagged rocks to leeward. Sally suggested that it would save our faces if we hoisted a notice to the effect that it was impossible to set our sail. The weight was later lifted from our souls as we saw the very yachtsmen who had given us scornful glances downstream drop their sails as soon as the wind grew fickle a mile or so below the town.

Lezardrieux appears to be a flourishing yachting centre with a large marina and two boat yards. Despite this, neither woodworking glue nor grip-fast nails were available and we had to buy Araldite at an astronomical price. With this and some nails (kindly supplied by Seton Campbell whom we found in the marina), I was able to set to work on the groove. By applying the glue, binding the mast securely with lengths of cord, then tightening the whole with a Spanish windlass, I hoped to effect a secure joint.

Friday, 24th August We decided to make for La Chambre on Ile de Bréhat, and it was then that I discovered that the crack in the luff groove extended further than I had previously thought, making it necessary to beat down the river under foresail alone. The gales were still blowing out at sea and we had a superb sail despite our lack of canvas. On the way downstream we were interested to see the beacons being painted in their new colours. We anchored in the entrance of La Chambre and once again set to work on the mast.

La Chambre dries out almost completely at low tide and many yachts are moored there permanently, resting on legs. We surveyed the harbour carefully at low tide and selected a suitable secluded spot to anchor. We moved in, put out the legs and turned in.

Saturday, 25th August At about 0300 we were woken by a sudden lurch to port and found ourselves slowly toppling over as the tide gushed out. What had appeared to be a sandy bottom was in fact thick mud covered by a thin covering of sand. We spent the next four hours dealing with our sideways world and the sludge which seeped in through the gunwales.

We remained in La Chambre that day, waiting for the gale to blow out and the boat to dry out. Our only voyage was down the harbour to a safer spot.

Sunday, 26th August In the early hours of the morning we had a repeat performance of the previous night, with the same mad scramble to get clothes, sleeping bags, cushions and food out of the water. It seems that the port-leg mounting had been weakened by the first incident, which caused it to flex inwards as the keel touched the sand.

At last the succession of gales which had kept us in port abated but we were too exhausted by our night of activity to make use of the fair weather, so we spent a happy day ambling round Bréhat. That night we anchored in the harbour entrance where the only way we could touch the bottom was by sinking. It was not such a bad spot after all.

Monday, 27th August The day dawned bright and sunny with a light north-westerly wind, so we departed by the easterly passage for St. Peter Port. It was high tide, which enabled us to cut across the outlying dangers, close hauled for Guernsey. We were shattered to hear on the radio of Lord Mountbatten's death at a time when we were having such a perfect day at sea.

By late afternoon we could see Guernsey but we were unable to make the course to St. Martin's Point on the south-east. As the wind dropped I gave in to Sally and we motored to our anchorage in Havelet Bay.

Tuesday, 28th August I woke to find a beautiful blue sky and a tall ship's rigging hanging over our hatchway. We emerged to find a three-masted French vessel rubbing her taffrail against our forestay. She had come in during the night and must have swung around on to us. A sleepy crewman stared down with complete lack of interest or concern. It transpired that he was the skipper and was not going to do anything about the situation, he was even surprised when we up-anchored and moved off. After stocking up with pints of delicious milk we set off for Herm. We approached the Rossière anchorage two hours before low water by way of the leading marks to the small harbour. As we beat towards the land, Sally kept a rock watch and swung the lead constantly. Local yachtsmen later asked us how we had managed to avoid all the outlying rocks. Indeed we were quite shocked at low water to find that there are many jagged rocks in an area that is quite blank on the latest chart. After a hot dusty walk around the island among the tourists, evening fell and all the visitors returned to Guernsey. Left alone we spent a pleasant night, although the noise of the strong current was rather disturbing – no wonder nobody else stayed the night.

Wednesday, 29th August We made a fast passage up to Alderney and entered Braye by way of the Swinge. At one point we sailed through an intersection of two currents flowing in opposite directions. It was a most disconcerting experience. For a few minutes the decks were completely submerged in the short waves and a little while after we were relieved to surf at high speed off the top of a wave into the harbour. There we found that the wind was coming up from the north-east, making a most uncomfortable swell, not only for our small boat but for all the larger ones too. On careful scrutiny during a walk round the harbour we noticed only one yacht floating in still water in the lee of Toulouse Rock. We moved hastily across the harbour, cooked and ate supper in comfort, while others – only a few yards off – pitched and tossed relentlessly. There was more than five feet of water at low tide and space for others to move in but nobody took advantage of the situation. We were able to rest well before sailing home the next day.

Thursday, 30th August We set sail at 0700 along with many others, on a course for the Needles. We made a slow start and picked up on a reach about mid-morning. *Harkaway* sailed well until mid-afternoon when the wind gradually faded and a fine mist descended. We wallowed for a while, enjoying the smooth sea and taking advantage of our 'sundeck'. It soon became apparent that the wind was not going to pick up for a while and we lamented that our outboard motor bracket had snapped the previous day. I constructed a cat's cradle around the motor, binding it to the remains of the bracket and the nearest stanchion. We suffered the motor for about four hours before we were able to take off on a reach again. By the early hours of the morning we were well within sight of the Needles' light and the tide was taking us rapidly east; it was a relief to pass the lighthouse into the Solent. The combination of tide and smooth Solent water gave us the most perfect sail we had had throughout the whole cruise. We finally dropped anchor outside Yarmouth harbour at 0330 on Friday, 31st August.

TABLE OF DISTANCES

		Distance made good	Time h.m.	Engine time h.m.
August				
18	Bembridge-Braye	74	16 00	0
20	Braye-Maseline	26	5 00	0
21	Maseline-Dixcart Bay	2	0 45	0
22	Dixcart Bay-Rade de Pommelin	46	14 45	1.30
23	Rade de Pommelin-Lezardrieux	5	1 30	1.30
24	Lezardrieux-La Chambre	5	1 30	0
27	La Chambre-Havelet Bay	44	13 20	1.20
28	Havelet Bay-Kossière	3	1 00	0
29	Kossière-Braye	42	5 00	0
30	Braye-Yarmouth	66	20 30	4.00
	Total Trip	313	79 20	8.20

AND MOTHER CAME TOO

by W.H.Batten

When Venetia Hayward first told her parents she was to be lent *Robertson's Golly* for the 1979 AZAB Race, her mother Stella was horrified, worried and thought Venetia was definitely mad. Had she been offered a chance to ride in the Grand National or at Badminton, Stella would have been delighted — such is the way of English horsey ladies.

Venetia has sailed on *Dyarchy*, our 27-ton Gaff cutter, from an early age and spent many long hours scrubbing, varnishing, and scraping her for us. Naturally we were not prepared to dissuade her from this splendid adventure. Instead, while out hunting one day in the winter, Sue my wife asked Stella to join us. We would leave with the race and hope to arrive in Ponta Delgado ready to welcome the *Golly*.

Plans had to be made fairly quickly. *Dyarchy* herself is in very good order after continuous attention from the family team during the last fifteen years, but the cosmetic side is never done and we were then waging a war on rust. This meant removing the stanchions and their fittings for re-galvanising and also any pieces from the running and standing rigging that did not have threads in them. The rest, bottle-screws etc., were painted with two coats of International two-pot metal primer, then two coats of galvaroid. The old genoa had blown out as we entered the Helford River at the end of 1978, so a new one was ordered. We also decided to invest in a secret weapon; a new deck-sweeping lightweight staysail such as the Falmouth working boats carry. This, with the genoa, proved a great success, pulling us to windward in light airs much faster than we had ever imagined.

It was a tight schedule to attend the champagne breakfast on *Golly* in Falmouth on Saturday, 2nd June, but we just made it, arriving with our daughter Bridget and her husband Angus on the beach at St. Just at 0330. The boat was ready on her mooring, stored and watered, and Stella was already there, having dined with Venetia the night before. After the breakfast party we motored into the easterly swell to watch the start. *Golly* supporters then had to be disgorged into unsuitable tiny dinghies and transferred to larger craft. Our dog was handed to our other daughter Tessa, ready for his London holiday. We made sail and proceeded to follow the race. It was the first time we had left the mooring this year, and there were still a few finishing touches to put to the rigging. By the time we settled down to enjoy our smoked salmon lunch (a present from Stella) we were going well and passing many of the smaller boats.

103

Golly set her spinnaker just before rounding the Lizard and disappeared into the murk ahead. We had one near miss with *Whisperer* when on the wind in light airs in the night, and that was the last we saw or heard of the race until we followed *Vashti* into Ponta Delgado on Tuesday, 12th June.

It was a marvellously easy passage. Unfortunately Stella was ill for two days and unable to help finish the smoked salmon. She actually allowed us to administer codeine, cough mixture and seasick pills in any order we chose. We set the yankee for one day but otherwise carried full sail to the genoa all the way. The booming-out pole which we had used when crossing the Atlantic had to have another lash up one evening.

There was the occasional jibe and a certain amount of playing with the headsails in the calms. The days passed very easily with the usual discussions about the menu, games of Scrabble, much use of the library, and the marvellous feeling that it was getting warmer. With St. Miguel in sight the wind became very light and variable, and eventually we resorted to the engine for short spells. At midnight, with Bridget on watch, the wind came and we sped around the south-east point.

On two consecutive days we met large French yachts. We spoke to one on the wireless (she was on passage to Gibraltar from the USA); the other altered course to talk to us but left it too late and could not catch us up. We were reaching fast and did not feel inclined to stop, even to speak to another cruising boat suddenly encountered in the ocean. We realised that our VHF has a very small range and we could rarely hear another yacht unless we could see her, so there was no possibility of keeping in touch with Venetia as her mother hoped. After the first few days we gave up trying.

We explored the town for two days before Venetia arrived with a large bunch of yachts that had all been becalmed off the island for twenty-four hours. Then followed a wonderful week of discovering the lovely island. The roadside verges are better than any English garden, the people extremely friendly and higher up in the mountains the hydrangea hedges complement meadows full of wild flowers that have mostly succumbed to sprays at home. We met lots of interesting and enthusiastic racing people and saw several extraordinary boats. There were one or two small things that Angus and I were able to do for Venetia but her engine defeated us and lost many people their bets.

On Wednesday, 20th June, we sadly left Stella ashore to fly home and motored well clear to watch the start. Eighty single- and double-handed yachts were virtually becalmed, moving in short bursts in strange directions. We started our engine occasionally just to keep out of the way of the competitors, but in the evening the wind came round the western end of the island and we were all away. In *Dyarchy* we stood on a bit to the north before turning for the Lizard which we reached nine days later after another fast sail. There was enough sun for navigating but certainly not enough for the crew returning to London, and it felt cold as we progressed north, mostly with a good beam wind. In fact, on 25th July, we broke our record for a day's run, logging 178 miles noon to noon. Before picking up our buoy at St. Just we couldn't resist sailing to Falmouth to see who was there. One Trimaran, *Whisky Jack, Stanford Mariner*, and one Contessa, *Cherry Valley Duck*, had beaten us — all of them maybe less than four years old. *Dyarchy* celebrated her fortieth birthday this year.

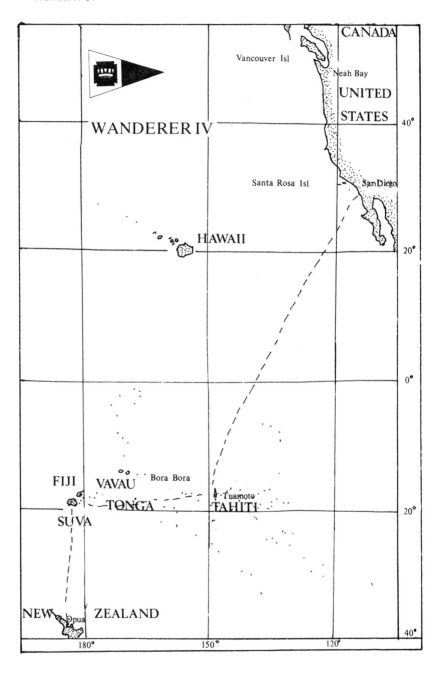

WANDERER IV: TO THE SOUTH PACIFIC AGAIN

by Eric Hiscock

Last summer Susan and I cruised in British Columbia, the lovely sheltered area, sprinkled with islands, that lies inside Vancouver Island.
We spent some time with Canadian friends Tom and Margaret Denny
(who knew the best places to go), they in *Daphne Isle* and we in *Wan-
derer IV*. We covered about five hundred miles, mostly under power
for there was hardly any wind. We shot through narrow passages
where the tide can run at up to twelve knots, saw snow-capped mountains and lumber camps, held a mini-meet (attended by Christopher
Pritchard-Barrett RCC who had flown out on business), and stopped
at thirty-five attractive anchorages. Some of these were overcrowded
and we might have avoided the crush by going further north, but we
did not go beyond Desolation Sound, partly because of lack of wind,
but chiefly because I was unable to see the many drifting logs or the
occasional deadhead in time to take avoiding action, so Susan had to
do all the steering or at least keep a constant lookout. (A deadhead is
a log, often of hemlock, up to seventy feet in length, so waterlogged
as to be almost entirely submerged and assuming a vertical attitude
with its upper end almost or completely awash.)

We returned with our friends to their own tiny island, which has
a house with shower, washing machine and bountiful water supply,
and a well-sheltered float with workshop and power tools, where they
helped us give our 49ft. steel ketch a much-needed refit. In October
we tucked ourselves away for the winter in a snug berth at Van Isle
Marina, near Sidney on Vancouver Island. The winter was severe
but, by living and sleeping in the saloon with the diesel-burning heater
going day and night, we managed to keep just warm enough. Many
people in the area were kind and hospitable, and Denis and Hilary
Swinburne and Ronnie and Lois Scott-Moncrieff (Denis and Ronnie
are long-standing members of the Club) did much to make our stay
easy, interesting, and enjoyable. The short and often gloomy days
passed quickly, and Susan and I agreed that we would not choose to
spend another winter afloat so far from the equator.

However, we left with many regrets at the end of April and as
there was no wind in the Strait of Juan de Fuca we put in at Neah
Bay on the US side to wait for some. It was as well that we did, for
bad weather followed. First there was torrential rain, accompanied
by the doleful moaning of foghorns, and then a hard southerly gale

during which fifty fishing vessels came in to shelter in our excellent anchorage.

We finally left on 8th May. Taking our departure from Cape Flattery we stood out to sea for sixty miles to avoid the shipping lanes and inshore fog and then turned south, keeping parallel with the coast. We started the passage with light winds, finished in a calm, and had a Force 8 north-westerly in the middle. We made the 1,005 miles to Santa Rosa Island (one of the more remote of the Channel Islands) in a week. We brought up in Becher Bay on the island's eastern side, where the homestead of the cattle ranch stands, and enjoyed a night of undisturbed sleep before continuing to San Diego.

Friends we had made on our visit nine years before looked after us splendidly during our twelve-day stay, and we departed under power in a calm to seek the fresh north-westerly wind which was reported to be blowing outside. However, it had blown itself out by the time we arrived and for the next eleven days we had overcast skies and long-lasting calms broken occasionally by light variable airs. Such weather is frustrating at any time, but it was particularly so just then because we wanted to get down to about 5°N before mid June. After this time there is some risk of hurricanes in the eastern part of the ocean, north of that latitude. Some may consider us over-apprehensive as very few storm tracks are shown on the pilot charts, but since the advent of meteorological satellites many more tropical storms have been reported in that wide and lonely area than in earlier days when, because of the lack of shipping, they may have formed and passed unnoticed. The Hawaiian radio station, WWVH, broadcasts time continually and gives Pacific weather warnings at forty-eight minutes past each hour; from that source we had news of the tropical storm Andreas and plotted her position each day. Fortunately for us she remained near the coast and finally turned inland. The next one, Bianca, crossed our track only a week after we had passed that way, and others followed.

At that time of year it is possible that the safer route to Tahiti (where we were bound) is via Hawaii, but that route adds a thousand miles to the total distance and would not have taken us into the northeast trade wind any faster than if we steered the direct course — which is what we did. On that course we should have found the trade in about 25°N; but we had to go much farther south than that before we at last reached it. The sky cleared and Susan was able to take her evening star sights. So brightly was the northern horizon illuminated by the full moon that, in 19°N and in the middle of the night, she was able to observe Polaris.

It was a joy to move along properly at last without having to bother with genoa and mizen staysail (the only sails to remain partially asleep in light airs when there is any swell) and to reel off about a thousand miles a week with the vane gear — which, like ourselves, prefers a good breeze — doing all the steering. The wind subsequently stayed with us carrying us through the belt where we might have expected doldrums; apart from a few showers there was no sign of them. The wind hauled round to a little south of east and continued to blow. Indeed, it blew rather hard and for a week we had reefs in main and mizen and the small jib set. The rhumb line from San Diego to Tahiti crosses the equator at 140°W, but we made our ninth crossing of the line a bit west of that so as to avoid the three vigias which lie near 140°W: two lots of 'breakers reported' and one patch of 'discoloured water', about which the *Pilot* is rather vague.

After that we steered to give the charted position of Mataiva (the westernmost atoll of the Tuamotu archipelago) a berth of ten miles and, as the latest determinations place the atoll five miles east of its charted position, we scarcely expected to see it. Yet we did see the tops of its palms, which was a great thrill after twenty-eight days out of sight of land. From there on only one danger lies in the northern approach to Tahiti: the unlighted atoll of Tetiaroa. Although we had had no worthwhile current so far on the passage there was a possibility of a strong west-setting current which has been the cause of more than one shipwreck, so we chose to pass to the west (to leeward) of the atoll and, after an orgy of navigation by sun and stars, we worked our way round it the following night, when it was very dark, with a headwind blowing at thirty-five knots and a rough sea. Later we sighted the loom of the lights of Papeete in the —by then— heavily clouded sky; instead of going straight there we stopped to rest for a couple of nights, after our 3,600-mile passage, at peaceful Moorea.

At Papeete, like all other yachts, we had to post a bond. For British yachts this is the equivalent of a thousand US dollars per person on board, while for Australian, New Zealand and US yachts it is five hundred dollars. The money is refunded at the final port of departure. (If the French invest this money until it is refunded, they must be doing pretty well with perhaps a hundred and fifty yachts in the group with an average of, say, four people aboard each.) We only remained at the noisy waterfront for two nights and then returned to enjoy a week's walking, swimming and meeting other voyagers on Moorea, a spectacularly mountainous island and one of the most lovely and least spoilt in the area.

Cruising among the Iles Sous de Vent was no fun because of lack of wind and the curiously steep and confused sea on which that great voyager, the late Tom Worth, remarked in the *Journal* of 1953. On leaving Bora Bora we had four days of proper and delightful trade-wind sailing, after which rain, calms, and some squalls of tremendous violence dogged us, and twelve days out we put in at Vava'u, an unsophisticated Tonga island with pleasant, dignified people, to effect temporary repairs to the wind-vane gear which had been damaged in one of the squalls. The weather was again unseasonable, with long-lasting calms and sometimes a headwind throughout the onward trip to Fiji, and I believe I am correct in saying that, with the exception of the four days I have mentioned, there was no trade wind in our part of the ocean throughout the entire months of July and August.

Since we first cruised in the South Pacific twenty-five years ago we have naturally seen some changes. Air travel has brought an invasion of tourists to change the islander's way of life and his attitude to visitors, but I do not believe that the ever-increasing number of voyaging yachts has done much harm (although port officials seem to think they have and treat them with suspicion) beyond choking the more popular anchorages and over-burdening the few facilities. Many yachts, particularly those from the USA, now make wide use of ship-to-shore or ham radio equipment, which often causes so much interference on the shortwave bands that others who are sharing the anchorages and also people living ashore are prevented from listening to the BBC, ABC, NZBC, and other stations. I am told that this is because the transmitters are defective (something to do with filters?), and it has become a tiresome nuisance. The attitude of port officials may hinge to some extent on the behaviour of recent arrivals. Racism is increasing and at Suva we were so abominably abused by an insolent immigration official, whose pleasure was to bait the British, that we will never again visit a port which, until this visit, had been a favourite of ours.

However, the great ocean swell still thunders on the coral reefs, the palm fronds wave and rustle in the breeze, and the nostalgic scents of wood-smoke, frangipane, copra, and rotting vegetation waft across the still lagoons along with traditional island sounds: the crowing of early morning roosters, the late night barking of dogs, and the occasional beat of drums and soft twang of guitars.

The final leg of the voyage, 1,100 miles to Opua in New Zealand, took thirteen days. We experienced one day of glorious sailing as we hurried through Kandavu Passage to take our departure from Cape Washington; but after that we had thunder, rain, calms and a gale from ahead, during which we lay hove-to under the close-reefed mainsail alone for eighty hours. We closed with the land by night in heavy rain, and at dawn found we had made a good landfall with the Cavalli Islands on the starboard bow and Cape Brett to port. As we made our way into the Bay of Islands, the sun came out to brighten the green landscape and the swell subsided.

Friends saw us coming up the channel from their house, broke out their largest flag and alerted the port officers, who this time were courteous and kind. Gifts of milk, fruit, and the day's paper were handed down from the wharf and by evening we were lying in the peaceful Waikare river on the mooring we had vacated eighteen months before.

THE 1979 FASTNET RACE

An Introduction by the Honorary Editor

The pages of the *Journal* and *Roving Commissions* are usually devoted to cruising under sail. Racing is well covered by the Royal Ocean Racing Club's magazine *Seahorse*.

The Fastnet Race this year provoked a feeling of great sadness for those who lost their lives, plus columns of questions and criticisms, tales of great courage and an opportunity to learn a little more about the sea, sailing and the design of yachts and equipment.

The following accounts are principally by people who usually cruise. Alain Catherineau's log is by invitation, for he has been awarded the Royal Cruising Club's seamanship medal. Finally, Clare Francis looks at the report of the RYA/RORC Fastnet Race Enquiry and adds her own thoughts.

Maldwin Drummond
Honorary Editor

JOLIE BRISE

by Robin Bryer

The 58-ton French-built pilot cutter *Jolie Brise* won the first, third and fourth Fastnet races under the flag of Commander E.G. Martin, a member of the Royal Cruising Club and founder of the Ocean Racing Club. Indeed *Jolie Brise* and Martin could reasonably be said to have invented British ocean racing in general and the Fastnet in particular.

Fifty-four years after her first triumph *Jolie Brise* found herself by chance on the fringe of the storm which made the 1979 race the most infamous of its otherwise distinguished history. I was bringing her home from Corunna with a crew of boys from Dauntsey's, my old school.

We were south-west of Ushant. Force 5 rose to Force 9 in half an hour. We lowered our gaff main downwind as the seas were already too steep to face – no small problem with thirty-eight feet of boom. That done, all hands were sent below. One boy watched from the companion way while either myself or my mate, fellow old-boy Colin Berry, helmed her through the night.

At 0400, when I was on watch, we were knocked down by a rogue sea. *Jolie Brise* recovered, shook herself like an old labrador, and took us on our way again. Just before dawn the lights of Ushant appeared comfortably on the starboard bow and we entered the English Channel. Fortunately it was only now that the gale veered to the west. We could still run before it in the right shipping lane along the French shore.

That night, in more moderate seas, we found ourselves south of the shipping lane and clear of the coast. Lights, occluded by the waves, hindered visual identification of our position, but a DF fix confirmed that it would be prudent to heave-to.

With one boy on watch, we had a comfortable night. After eggs and bacon, we hoisted the main, sailed north to cross the shipping lanes at right angles, and then set course for Poole.

The BBC was making us all too aware of the disasters to the north of us, all the more distressing because the father of one boy was skippering a Fastnet boat. Only later was his safety confirmed.

Throughout this adventure the spirit of E.G. Martin himself seemed to be with us. I had just read his book *Deep Water Cruising*, published in 1928, of which *Jolie Brise* herself is the heroine. Time and again his phrases came back to me. '*An auxiliary is useful when there is a flat calm and there are ladies on board,*' Martin had written. We had one lady on board but it was certainly not a flat calm when I switched the engine on to regulate the speed to keep us either with or ahead of the waves.

'*In the Fastnet Race of 1925 I lowered my mainsail altogether.*' On this occasion I had done the same with Martin's words almost ringing in my ears.

'*In a really good sea boat a gale may be a time of rest rather than of hardship for the crew.*' It certainly seemed it — at least when I left the hell on deck to find the London-club calm below. Even after we were knocked down, the worst I heard was a plaintive cry from Maureen our cook, dressed in her best nightie, asking if anyone had seen her handbag. The added comfort of having my clothes dried on the Esse, warm and ready for the next watch, was paralleled by the helmsman in one of *Jolie Brise*'s modern counterparts having his hat sent down for warming in the microwave oven. The ease of a vessel of over fifty feet was and always will be amazingly greater than that of smaller fry.

'*Ocean voyages can, of course, be made in yachts which are far smaller,*' Martin conceded, but the equation of comfort with safety and size formed a major part of his creed and I can now see why.

I had had fears about the spars and rigging, towering above me vibrating '*like the strings of an enormous double bass*' (another Martin phrase). But '*inherent strength*' was what Martin put his trust in. '*It is not the force of the wind which does damage but the violence of the motion and to withstand this an elastic structure is better than a rigid one. . . . The mast should take some of the strain before the rigging comes fully into play. . . . The spring in hemp lanyards eases the shock upon the hull of the ship.*' Antiquated ideas maybe, but what Martin called 'Marconi' masts and bottle-screws fared ill in the storm to the north of us that night.

'*The long-keeled ship with a good forefoot has an immense advantage*' — if it is not immune from being knocked down, as we discovered, such a ship is certainly quick to recover and marvellous when hove-to.

'*Bulwarks are . . . invaluable in sea going craft. In* Jolie Brise *they measure two feet from the deck to the top of the rail and . . . no one who has sailed in her will forget the sense of security and the comfort which they give on deck.*' Indeed we will not. It was the bulwarks which meant that after we had rounded Ushant, we could sun ourselves quite safely on the fore-deck, even though the helmsman might still occasionally be up to his waist in water at his position at the lowest point of her freeboard.

But although *Jolie Brise* is traditional in the extreme, E.G. Martin was no reactionary. '*That he is racing can never be any justification for a skipper risking life,*' he might claim, but the winner of the 1926 Fastnet earned Martin's respect even though he had three men overboard at one time. '*I believe that, in time, we shall see the development of a class of yachts more efficient than those which have hitherto been built,'* even allowing for the predominance of bottle screws and the absence of bulwarks, I think he would consider his prophecy fulfilled today.

'The weather during the 1927 Fastnet Race was abominable. There were some who regarded it as a catastrophe; to me it seemed the reverse . . . and it was proved beyond doubt that the course is a safe one. No committee is justified in sending yachts over a really dangerous course and in the weather then, which is as bad as it is ever likely to be, every vessel reached harbour in safety although many were disabled' – if only that were as true of the 302 yachts which competed in 1979 as it was of the little fleet of fifteen of which he was then writing.

'It is well known that racing design . . . has a marked effect on that of cruising yachts,' Martin went on to write. *'To me it seems not at all a foolish hope that the ocean racing yachts of the future may set a standard which will bring an improvement in the form of cruising yachts.'* I think he was right, and that is why I respect those racing men who fared so much worse than we did on that fateful night of 13th August 1979.

But respect and envy are poles apart. To be out of the centre of the storm and in Martin's old boat, rather than in some extreme evolution of what he and she stood for, was close enough for me.

When I look back to last summer, it is to my son William playing on the beach at Sark with our own *Frisk* lying off shore, or to *Jolie Brise* anchored beneath the eucalyptus-lined slopes of some distant Spanish ria. The gale I can forget. My sympathy is with those who never will.

AUTONOMY

by Matthew and Frances Power

After two easy and very slow Fastnets, it came as a great shock to those not taking part to learn of the terrible 'storm that devastated the racing fleet. Twenty-three yachts were either abandoned or sunk and seventeen yachtsmen lost their lives. It was the worst ocean racing disaster there has ever been and its effect will be felt for many years to come.

Frances and I were kindly given berths for the race on board *Autonomy* belonging to Edward Bourne our Honorary Secretary. *Autonomy* is the first of a 36ft. Red Admiral class designed by Holman & Pye as a fast competitive cruiser racer, built by Buchan Yachts and launched in 1979. She has accommodation for up to seven and a big saloon and separate aft cabin. *Autonomy* seemed enormous after *Pennyroyal* and we all lived very comfortably. The rig is the optional three-quarter with runners, a cap shroud and a lower shroud each side. A babystay, a forestay and a hydraulic backstay make up the rest of the rigging. The large wardrobe of headsails for the varying wind conditions includes three genoas and a storm jib, three spinnakers, a big buoy and a trisail. *Autonomy* is a fast boat under all combinations of sail, but we found her overmasted and underballasted in strong winds which caused her to be tender when on the wind.

We were, however, very lucky to be on such a well-built and dependable boat; nothing structural gave way and there was no serious damage to the mast or rudder, both common casualties on other boats. The storm only caused superficial damage: the boom and guardrail stanchion were bent during the knockdown; the mast was slightly bent above the crosstrees; and one of the spinnaker booms, its deck fittings, the dan buoy, helmsman's seat, and radar reflector were all lost.

All the navigational instruments were ruined except for the Homer Heron RDF, and all the wiring has had to be replaced. The instruments at the mast-head disintegrated and the mast-collar at the deck disappeared. The rigging appeared to be very slack, although – strangely – we found nothing wrong back in port.

Autonomy was fully fitted with the safety equipment required by the RORC, including an eight-man liferaft, two liferings, dan buoy, a Verey pistol, and various different flares. There was also a VHF radio set, but it was saturated after the knockdown and was useless afterwards. Since our return it has had to be replaced.

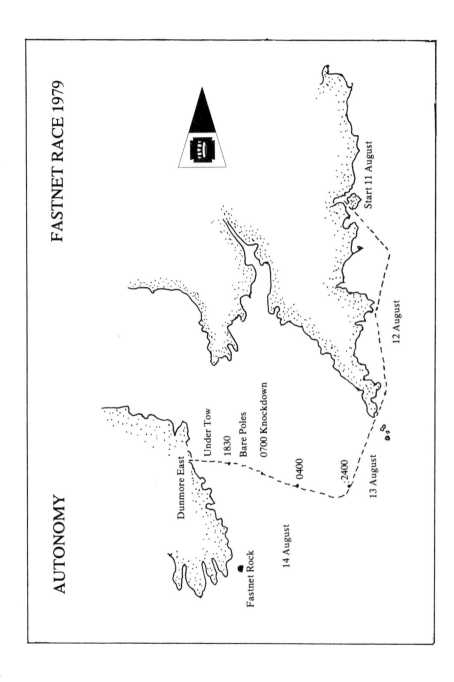

Autonomy

116

As a crew we all got on together famously considering our various different experiences in sailing. Between us we had all sailed many thousands of miles in racing dinghies, offshore racers and cruising yachts. We were a mixed bunch but it provided plenty of scope for conversation. During the gale there was no panic, everyone went about his or her task as if there was nothing seriously wrong. Morale remained surprisingly high and we all chatted and joked about the smallest things, but later back in port over a glass of Guinness we all admitted how frightened we had been at the time. Edward, unfortunately, was prevented from coming on the race at the last minute in spite of having painstakingly chosen such a good crew. His place was taken by Simon Skey and it is to his superb seamanship we owe our lives: if it had not been for him we would not be here to write this.

The people of Dunmore East were very hospitable to us and we owe them a debt we can never properly repay; throughout our short stay there we were constantly invited out and helped by many kind people. After completing numerous small repairs, such as tightening the rigging and clearing up the shambles below, we left for Lymington with many regrets and with every intention to return. Frances' account of the race follows.

The Fastnet race of 1979 will always be remembered as a terrible tragedy. For those of us who escaped relatively unscathed, however, it was, in retrospect, a marvellous experience – but not one to be repeated. For Matthew and me it was a baptism by fire into off-shore racing, and I certainly viewed the race with trepidation, convinced that I would never be able to 'grind a winch' fast enough or change a headsail in under a minute! I found that being female was definitely to my advantage – you are not shouted at so much when something goes wrong.

There were eight of us in the crew: four were very experienced ocean racers, the rest cruising people. We cruisers toned down the almost hysterical sailing of the racing men, while the racing men jolted the cruisers out of our lethargy. It later became apparent to me that, in our case, this combination produced a very strong crew.

On Saturday, 11th August the race began. Class III started at 1350 and with a westerly wind of fifteen knots we had a very exciting beat to the Needles, at which point the larger boats who had had a later start were bearing down on us at great speed. Throughout Sunday we sailed in thick fog and on Monday, 13th August at 1200 we rounded Land's End very fast in a south-westerly of about twenty-five knots. The 1835 forecast that evening, 'S4 locally 6, increasing 6 – 8 from NW later', was received well and we looked forward to a decent wind. Under 1.5 Triradial spinnaker and full main, *Autonomy* was going like a train. After an enormous stew for supper the watch on entertained

AUTONOMY'S BAROGRAPH TRACE DURING FASTNET

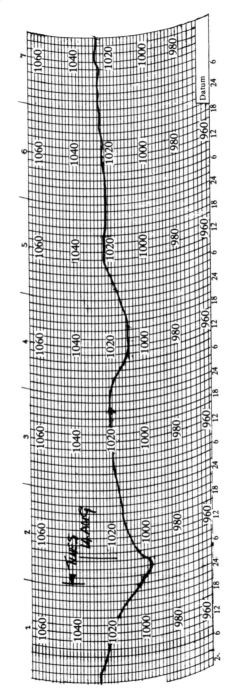

The vertical line directly under the u in Tues was caused by the knockdown.

Note: The barograph was over-reading

the watch below with a selection of songs. At about 2100 the port
spinnaker snap-shackle broke and the spinnaker was rehoisted on the
starboard halyard; also two slabs were taken in the main. By 2200 the
wind was increasing and we handed the spinnaker and hoisted No. 2
jib; even then we had the storm jib up within an hour. At midnight we
took a third slab in the main and settled down to our four-hour watch.
The latest forecast was not encouraging, 'SSW veering W 7/9 locally,
10 in Fastnet'. However, we were well fed and at that point reasonably
warm. By 0015, however, the wind was gusting over fifty knots and
with a lot of trouble we got the main down (in a strong wind sails
certainly have a mind of their own). The seas were already large, with
breaking crests; it was rather like being in a roller coaster with the
added terrors of a ghost train! I was not looking forward to daylight
and actually seeing those enormous waves. The noise of the wind in
the rigging was deafening and for those of us on watch at that time
talking was impossible. We retreated into our oilskins and took it in
turns to sit on the cockpit floor – a very comfortable place as one
didn't have to brace oneself against the continuous rolling. By 0300
we had had enough and watches were changed to two hours because the
incessant buffeting and noise of the wind was physically and mentally
exhausting.

By 0330 we were bailing fast. Occasional seas were breaking over the
decks and the cockpit was continually filling up, and the water somehow found its way down below. (We were later to find that this was
due to the cockpit lockers.) The two bilge pumps were unable to cope
so buckets were brought into action and passed up through the main
hatch, while one person was seen bailing the cockpit with a pint mug!

The barograph was quite spectacular: it had fallen thirty millibars in
twenty-six hours. (I hear that on another boat a crew member suggested
putting a matchstick under the barograph arm to keep it high.) At
about 0430, now nearly light, we spotted a yacht close astern and
managed to raise them on the VHF. It turned out to be yacht *Locomotion* and after a short chat we wished them luck and signed off.
They had been able to get a fix and estimated our position as 50°
50'N 7°51'W. They soon disappeared in the murk, but it was cheering
to know that they were not far away.

Bailing continued, a very strenuous task and a good way of keeping
warm. I found that as long as I was doing something I did not have
time to be frightened. By now it was daylight and 'dawn revealed a
ghastly scene'. The sea and the sky were varying shades of grey and
visibility was not good. At 0615 the skipper radioed to the *Overijssel*
and reported that we were taking in water faster than we thought we
could manage and gave the position that *Locomotion* had given us
earlier that morning. We had been pooped twice in the last hour and the
water in the cabin was rather deep. During one of the poopings the
dan buoy had broken free and was now lashed to the deck; the boom

was lashed to the guard rail. The stern was very low in the water and there was at least six inches of water on the cabin sole.

At 0710 we were knocked down. Three of us were down below manning the bilge pump, listening to the radio and passing buckets to Julian who was standing in the main hatch. The other four were in the cockpit. Water poured through the main hatch and I remember doing a full backward somersault that ended on the chart table with the skipper on top of me. The cabin was in total chaos. On deck it was even worse. Two of the four crew there had been washed over the stern and were, as they put it, water-skiing; luckily their lifelines held and they were soon back on board. The other two were entangled in the guard rails. Matthew had crashed into Andrew en route and both had ended up plaited in the rails. Andrew had badly injured his leg but still remarked humorously that he had taken up off-shore racing because he was fed up with capsizing dinghies!

We were now so full of water that the two who had gone over the stern had been able to reach the top rail of the pushpit from the water. Bailing — with any vessel we could find — continued at a furious rate. The bilge pump in the cockpit was now broken, but the secondary pump in the cabin was still OK. The water level in the cabin was up to the navigator's seat, and the cabin itself was cluttered with saucepans, clothes, cutlery, bottles of Scotch and a host of other floating debris. The VHF had got wet and was now useless. Up in the cockpit anything loose had gone, including the helmsman's seat and the dan buoy, which had disappeared in pieces. On deck the spinnaker pole fittings had been ripped out of the deck and the masthead fittings were useless and hung drunkenly.

By 0730 we had the storm jib down and we streamed warps astern. In the heat of the moment one of the warps had been thrown to windward and it jammed in the rudder. However, the boat's motion was easing, the cockpit drier, and the water in the cabin shallower. With the last dry match the cooker was lit and we all had some soup. At 0810 I saw a ship and we sent off a red flare. It was not seen. This was not surprising: unless both boats were on the crest of a wave at the same moment, it was impossible to see anything. By 0815 we had completed bailing and started a system of two on watch for two hours each. Except for the watch, we retired to our sodden bunks.

Although the sea and wind were not all that cold, we found it difficult to keep warm. My oilskin jacket had ripped and I was soaked to the skin; in fact no one was all that dry. However, wet clothes under oilskins work on the wet-suit principle and are reasonably warming. Sharing bunks was another good way of getting warm and this caused a few ribald comments as I was the only woman on board. Morale was amazingly high and for some unknown reason we were all imitating the accents of Inspector Clouseau of the Pink Panther films. Even the most inane comment was considered a huge joke and, as the day dragged on, spirits rose despite our situation.

At mid-day I went on watch for two hours, a boring, tiring duty. We could not steer and there was nothing to do except keep a look out for ships or planes. Julian and I discussed ways in which we wanted to be rescued. He wanted it to be by a helicopter, because he had never been in one; I wanted to be picked up by a ship full of handsome Frenchmen. At about 1300 a plane flew very low across our bows and we fired a Verey flare. The plane made no sign that it had seen us and flew off. However, we felt better for having seen it and found out later that it had in fact spotted us.

The afternoon dragged on. The skipper had managed to get a sun sight at noon – not an easy task considering the weather; this put us at about 51° 20.8′N. The wind was moderating all the time but the sea was not. During the afternoon we ate some muesli with hot milk and about ten spoons of sugar each, not a very appetising dish, but this, with Mars bars and bananas was all that we could manage in our predicament. The Mars bars were tremendous – we ate forty-eight in three and a half days. Bananas were also good, as they were easy to eat. We even used the skins to make a 'floral' arrangement in a mug in an effort to brighten up the cabin!

By 1815 the wind had moderated enough for us to hoist one third of the storm jib in an effort to give a positive direction, hopefully towards Dunmore East at the entrance to Waterford harbour. Dunmore East seemed to be where we were heading. By this time the skipper was navigating on a very wet chart using a plastic knife and fork, all the other instruments having mysteriously disappeared!

At about 1830 a shout went up from the cockpit 'They're here.' The Dunmore East lifeboat was steaming towards us at great speed; even so we sent up some Verey flares to make damn sure they saw us. They told us that we were some thirty miles SSW of Dunmore East and they would escort us in. After about twenty minutes they offered us a tow because speed under storm jib was slow and we were unable to steer; this was an offer we gladly accepted. We hadn't risked hoisting any more sail as the rigging was very slack. Three other yachts also appeared and with the most beautiful sunset to port we all headed for Dunmore East.

We couldn't believe the welcome we received on our arrival in the early hours of Wednesday morning. Within an hour of mooring we had all had hot showers and were safely ensconced in the Yacht Club, sandwiches in one hand, Guinness in the other. The generosity of the inhabitants of this small town seemed endless and, for the next few nights, we were all guests of various families. One resident of Dunmore East commented: 'We havn't had so much fun since the Bell Rock disaster.' All I can say is thank God, the St. Patrick lifeboat, the Irish and, most of all, *Autonomy*, that we got there at all.

Postscript *by Edward Bourne*

Autonomy was luanched on Friday, 17th February 1979. As my wife Penny launched *Autonomy* critics of modern yacht design will have delighted in the similarity in shape of my wife and my yacht: Penny was within weeks of producing baby Thomas.

Throughout the spring and early summer we carried out modifications to *Autonomy*; being the first of her class, there were as many problems to solve as there would be with a one-off design. However, it is to the credit of the designers, Holman & Pye, the builders, and the marketing company that the difficulties were persistently and cheerfully ironed out. Interestingly enough, it was at this early stage that we had 350lb. of lead taken off the keel because *Autonomy* was felt to be over-ballasted. Matthew Power is quite right in saying that this was a mistake.

In July we spent three delightful weeks sailing from Salcombe down to Vigo, then on to Oporto and returning via the Rias to Ireland for the Joint Meet. We used this time to spot and rectify a few more teething troubles.

When choosing the design I did not have racing in mind. It has always been my view that there is no particular merit in going slowly for the sake of it, and I feel that for all the harm the IOR rule is reputed to have done to yacht design, it is true that speed and also the standard of accommodation have been improved by the trends of yacht design over the last ten years (excluding the extremes). *Autonomy* was conceived simply as a boat in which one could cruise comfortably to areas which would be inaccessible on a three-week holiday in a slower boat. The choice of rig deserves some comment here. In racing circles the current trend away from mast-head rig is regarded as radical; but to those brought up with cruising designs it is simply a common-sense way of reducing the area of sails which has to be handled. The effect of the three-quarter rig is that one must be prepared to reef the mainsail sooner and more frequently; but any task is considerably less arduous than it would be otherwise. The racing fraternity regard *Autonomy* as very heavily built, but it is probably truer to say that she is of a modern design with the normal scantlings and displacement of a conventional cruising yacht. This is certainly one of the main reasons why she survived the Fastnet relatively undamaged.

The lessons which I have learnt are primarily concerned with over-sophistication. From the central heating to the instruments and from the hydraulics to the hot water system, the hostile environment of heavy weather will always win. If *Autonomy* had been fitted out more simply and with fewer gadgets, the repairs necessary after her knock-down would have been relatively trivial. As it was, the operation of replacing what the Americans in Ireland so charmingly and picturesquely described as 'mast-head broccoli' – with all its associated wiring and installation – has been a long and complicated one which is only now nearing completion as I write. Apart from the mast, which was slightly bent, and the other damage referred to by Matthew and Frances, the other problems were all internal and involved damage to the varnish-work, upholstery and above all the electrics. A point of some interest here is the batteries. These were of the new Freedom type and amazingly survived submersion, but many owners will probably now give thought to better protection of their alternator, or carrying a spare, and means of coping with power and a lost mast-head aerial. The two most important changes which I shall make to *Autonomy* will be to the cockpit lockers, which although capable of being locked shut, nonetheless failed to prevent water getting below, and the main bilge pump, which was of a hopelessly flimsy design. To be fair, one of the crew was actually pumping when he was swept overboard and took with him the handle and some of the pump.

In all, I feel that there are some aspect of design – notably sail area to displacement ratio – which make *Autonomy* lively, or perhaps one should say hard work, to sail, but there is absolutely no evidence that either her beam (11ft. 3in. on an overall length of 36ft. 2in.) or her fin keel in any way contributed to her being knocked down. This is clearly a debate which will rage for a while to come and it is not my intention, other than making the above observations, to attempt to draw any conclusions. I feel that also beyond dispute is the fact that as Matthew and Frances have indicated, the strength of the yacht's construction greatly benefited crew morale and minimised damage.

I cannot finish this postscript without paying tribute to the seamanship of all on board. As soon as I heard that *Autonomy* had been in trouble and had arrived in Ireland, I made arrangements to fly out and bring her back. When I arrived I found the entire crew in high spirits and dedicated to putting matters right. By the time I arrived in Dunmore East, *Autonomy* already looked as if she had suffered nothing worse than a normal gale. It was greatly to the credit of the crew that all of them, except for those with urgently beckoning offices, wanted to sail back to England in the boat.

SARIE MARAIS

by David Gay

Sarie Marais is a 33ft. cruiser/racer (Maica class), designed by Illing-worth & Primrose and built by Attrills in 1961. Her 6ft.-deep keel gives her a good performance in heavy weather, particularly to wind-ward. She was purchased from the Royal Marines Sailing Club in 1969 and since then has cruised and raced from Bergen to Santander in all weathers up to gale strength. She is fitted with conventional cruising and off-shore racing equipment but without VHF, radio telephone, or wind instruments.

She has missed only one Fastnet race, in 1973, when she was cruis-ing in Holland.

Sarie Marais' crew of six were all members of — or closely associated with — the Sea Cadet Corps, except for Brian who had stepped in two days before the race to replace someone who had dropped out at the last minute. With the exception of the skipper, the crew's ages ranged from twenty to twenty-eight. Unusually, four out of the six of us had also been trained in square-rig. David (mate) and Ged (second mate) had both been on the previous Fastnet, a light-winded marathon in which *Sarie* had finished at 0600 on the Sunday. All in all it was a powerful, cheerful and seaman-like crew; a crew that proved to be remarkably humorous and strong of stomach in the days to follow. No one showed the slightest sign of *mal de mer* on the race; perhaps Stu-geron assisted the more susceptible members of the crew.

As skipper, I considered myself very fortunate to have the backing of such a team, particularly the mate, Lieutenant David Comer, who, quiet and unflappable, was a tower of strength at all times.

Only three and a half days before the start of Fastnet, I was still aboard *Royalist*, battling back from the Fowey-Isle of Man race in the teeth of a southerly Force 6. I turned over *Royalist* at Fishguard twenty-four hours behind schedule and then travelled by car to Lym-ington, where *Sarie's* crew had gathered to store and scrub off at Lymington Town quay. There was a work-up race at Cowes, which David skippered on Friday, while I was catching up on paperwork and domesticity, and then we were off at 1330 on Saturday, 11th August. I felt in fine form after ten days of STA racing in the Irish Sea, and I was certainly tuned in to the weather pattern!

The opening phase of the race was an uneventful beat down the Channel in light winds and moderate/poor visibility. The exception was

124

when we stood by a French Class II boat, whose carbon fibre rudder had broken in the Portland Race; the Weymouth lifeboat arrived just in time for us to take the last of the tide past the Bill.

Just after 1600, Monday the 13th, we sighted Long Ships at only eight-cables range and set course for the Rock. Shortly after, one of the more optimistic members of my crew reported a Class I boat in company. This was, in fact, returning from the Fowey-Isle of Man race.

The 1750 forecast gave gale warnings for all south-western areas; and the sky, a heavier swell than normal and the barometer falling fifteen millibars between 0600 and 1800 all indicated what was to come. Meanwhile, we were reaching before a SSW 3/4 under a large genoa and full mainsail.

From 2200 on Monday things moved very fast indeed for us. By then the wind had veered to WSW and we were close fetching under full sail. The wind and sea increased relentlessly and we were forced to change down to No. 3 genoa; ten minutes later I wished it had been the working jib. At the midnight change of watch we took off the mainsail, as we were now experiencing a good Force 6 and the seas were building fast. Even under No. 3 genoa alone, *Sarie* was making six to seven knots and laying easily to windward of the rhumb line. I was, of course, keeping an EP, confirmed by reasonable DF bearings on Round Island and St. Mawgan Air Beacon. I had taken over the watch myself and for an hour we had a breathing space, but the wind was still rising and the sea, getting up very rapidly, was very steep and beginning to break.

Suddenly the boat staggered under a massive onslaught of water and seemed momentarily overwhelmed. We had been going too fast and must have slipped into the trough and then into the next wave. The cockpit was filled to the coamings, and I felt just as if I had capsized a dinghy – only here it was a long way to shore. Fortunately the washboards had remained in place, and there was no apparent damage and no water below.

The stand-by watch was called on deck and we shifted down to storm jib, still continuing our course to the north-west. The mate's watch took over at 0300, and the rest of us went below to lie on our bunks fully clothed in our oilskins. We did not have long to wait for the next act in the drama. At about 0330 there was an enormous crash as *Sarie* fell off another wave. This quickly forced me from my bunk, only to be assaulted over the left temple by a jar of marmalade hurtling from the galley shelf. Clearly we were still going too fast, albeit under storm jib. We were just to weather of rhumb line and some thirty-seven miles north of the Scillies with at least forty miles of sea room in hand; in view of this I decided that the best course of action was to lay a-hull.

It was a blood-stained skipper that relieved the mate on the helm. The yacht was temporarily run off to provide a stable platform for'd for the watch on deck to claw down the storm sail, which they did valiantly. It was now blowing Force 9/11 (we had no wind instruments, but this figure has since been established from Met. reports) and the seas were very steep, breaking and still building. However, they did not appear to be as vicious or 'rogue' as they seem to have been further north. To my intense relief, my two fore-deck heroes returned to the cockpit unscathed, and the yacht lay a-hull with main boom secured inboard and tiller lashed well to leeward.

A sense of comparative peace descended over our boat and crew. We lay quite comfortably sixty degrees off the wind; we never tacked through the crests or fell away. Two crew members remained on watch to keep a look out for other craft and assess weather changes. Their safety harnesses were at short scope, passed through winch supports and clipped to own parts, and washboards were in place.

Occasionally a wave broke inboard with considerable force, but we were never knocked down beyond sixty degrees and my only concern now was whether the rig and the chain plates would stay the course.

At about 1000, Tuesday the 14th, the wind moderated to about Force 8/9, although the seas were still enormous. Sitting in the cockpit was like being on a roller-coaster ride around Alpine peaks but somehow had a strange fascination. I served breakfast of hot Bovril and biscuits and spirits began to rise. The mate and I then tackled the chore of bleeding the diesel of air, which must have entered the engine at some stage during the previous twenty-four hours, as when we started the engine to charge, nothing had happened. By noon we had the engine going and the after-guard celebrated with a tot!

During the forenoon a Nimrod had flown over us, and she presumably homed HMS *Anglesey* on to us. The foremast-head of this Fishery Protection ship was lost at times behind the crests as she came near, making the whole scene reminiscent of a Western Approaches' war-time operation in bad weather. I judged the sea height to be between thirty and thirty-five feet. *Anglesey* positioned herself expertly on our lee quarter and dangled a lifebelt from the wings of the bridge. We released her with a thumbs-up signal and *Anglesey* went on her way. We later learned that she had previously recovered the entire crew of another yacht, left abandoned some eight miles to the north-west of *Sarie*.

We were shocked to hear on the BBC one o'clock news of all the founderings and drownings among our competitors. Then three hours later, in a fast moderating wind and sea, I had finally to decide whether to continue the race or retire. On one hand we had a strong, non-seasick crew — four of whom wished to continue — and there was no damage; on the other hand there was still three hundred and fifty miles to go, our anxious relatives including a wife who was expecting a baby in four weeks' time and other crews' lives already lost, plus a massive SAR operation in progress which we did not wish to complicate by a late finish. With regret, we hoisted the working jib at 1600 and set a course of a hundred and forty degrees. This took us within one mile of Longships, where we met some of the Admiral's Cup boats on their final leg.

Sarie berthed at Millbay Docks at 1630 to an unexpected flurry of public interest. We learned later that only one out of the fifty-eight boats in our class (Class V) had finished, while six yachts had been abandoned, two sunk and three lives lost. We were all stunned by the emotional reunion with our own relatives and did not appreciate their agonising experience until we saw some very harrowing scenes on television and in the press and learned that *Sarie* had also been 'unaccounted for'. We felt rather humble by the experiences of other boats and the many acts of heroism.

Two days later my cheerful race crew – who have all promised to come back in 1981 – were relieved by a family crew at Dartmouth. *Sarie* then proceeded quietly and rather sadly to Brittany for a conventional summer cruise.

Lessons learned from the tragic Fastnet

1 It would appear that a long deep keel configuration stands up well to such conditions.

2 In our case, and in the conditions we experienced, lying a-hull seemed to work very well, although we probably did not experience the worst seas. It was also used successfully by *Maid of Malham* and *Theta* in the previous stormy race – the 1956 Channel race. *Maid of Malham* did however suffer some damage.

3 Leeway, while lying a-hull, seems to have only been about one and a half knots.

4 VHF might have helped to report our position and relax our relatives but the Mayday traffic on Channel 16 would not have been good for crew morale. However, on balance, I accept any future insistence that it should be fitted.

5 Our stormsail is too big.

6 Doses of Stugeron ensured that the two potentially seasick members of our crew did not succumb.

LORELEI

by Alain Catherineau

We were racing with fifty knots of wind, using the No. 4 jib and with three reefs in the Hood mainsail. At about 0200 (French time), 14th August, we were sailing at 310° at ninety degrees apparent wind, our speed was considerable and below decks there was a constant impression that we were surfing. Thierry, my first mate, was at the helm, taking great pleasure in the almost effortless sailing; the boat was standing up well and quite stable. Towards 0230 we were thirty or forty miles from Fastnet and well on course. After about a mile we set the star-cut; shortly afterwards, with an apparent thirty or thirty-five knots, we replaced this, first with the No. 2 and then with the No. 4. For about an hour we passed many boats, both windward and leeward of us.

Suddenly we were astonished to see a red parachute flare about half a mile downwind. I donned my harness and rushed forward and with the help of Marc and Gerard, the navigator, hauled down the No. 4. I had been prepared for this: the wind was remarkably gusty and our anemometer was recording up to sixty knots. Thierry and I decided to get closer to the red light; with three reefs in the mainsail it was easy for us to steer towards it. After failing on the first try, we finally went about. We were heading roughly south, Thierry still at the helm, when we saw a rocket or a red hand-held flare (I can no longer remember which). We could not see the source of the light, only a red halo that was visible from time to time above the waves. I asked Thierry to stop heading towards the glow and ease off by about thirty degrees; we had no idea what sort of boat we would find. Some hours earlier we had met *Rochelais*, a rusty French trawler from La Rochelle, a most impressive sight. For some reason I thought that the crew in difficulty now was on a fishing boat.

We were very comfortable below deck; however, on deck, we would have lost two or three crewmen had not our harnesses been well-fitted. We were still heading towards the light when we saw two smaller lights above something dark; these were in the same wave and about fifty metres downwind. It was a liferaft. Some way farther on we turned and headed towards the liferaft, our mainsail at three reefs. We came three metres upwind of it, the same distance away from it and at a speed of about three knots. One of my crew threw a rope to the liferaft, but it would not reach. Two of the liferaft's crew hurled themselves towards us in an attempt to catch the hull; instead they fell into the sea and were hauled back by their colleagues.

I decided to take over the helm. I felt it was possible to save these men as long as I was at the helm and an integral part of my boat. I know *Lorelei* very well and can often demand—and get—the impossible. I started the engine and hauled down the mainsail. The engine is a twelve horse power diesel, but the propeller has automatic variable pitch which gives maximum power very quickly and greater than normal acceleration and deceleration. After seven or eight unsuccessful attempts I finally managed to come about and headed into the wind. During this time we had covered some distance. We were heading south, in total darkness, in search of the red light. Suddenly we saw it. I turned again — an easier job than it had been the first time — and cautiously headed towards the red glow, which lit up the surrounding blackness whenever it became visible. I turned to the north and crossed at about four or five knots. I approached the liferaft and aimed *Lorelei* straight at it when we were about twenty-five metres away. I threw the engine into reverse in the last few metres and thanks to *Lorelei*'s propeller of variable pitch, she drew rapidly to a halt, stopping within a metre of the liferaft.

Thierry and Marc each threw a line to the raft and the crew hauled themselves alongside *Lorelei*. I felt dead. There was some confusion on the liferaft as the crew leaped to catch hold of our ropes or deck. One or two climbed aboard easily; three more remained in our stern on the aluminium toe-rail. I suddenly noticed that the liferaft was drifting away from us with two of the crew still on board. Luckily one of them managed to grasp a rope that had stayed on board and pulled the raft back alongside. A few moments later the liferaft drifted away, empty. The end of the rope had not been made fast. I stopped the motor for safety and some of my crew helped two men climb aboard and three or four more of us at the stern helped the remaining three. The first few castaways were already in the cabin; there were only two left in the sea and we were having difficulty getting them aboard.

I sent the fit members of the liferaft crew to help out on deck. I was holding on to one who had been under the counter with only his head above water. He was one of the few to have a harness and I managed to pass a rope through it and then over the pushpit. In this way I lifted him out of the water. However, the harness slipped over his shoulders and I had to release him into the water again. Philippe was holding him by his T-shirt, the only garment he had. Finally, helped by his fellow English crew members, the castaway was rescued from the waves. He was heavy and it took five or six heaves on the ropes to pull him into the cockpit.

In the cockpit his leg became trapped between two ropes, but we soon released him. The most injured member of the English crew was forward but there was still one more in the sea. I can no longer remember how we finally rescued him. I think that *Lorelei*, crossing the waves, heeled on the right side, sometimes very severely, so that we could grip the last castaway and haul him in a few centimetres. He was stiff with cold and could not help us rescue him. Soon he was in the cockpit surrounded by his rescuers. I realised that there was something wrapped around his head; he was being strangled by a cord on his T-shirt. I pulled at it with all my strength and it finally snapped. He was taken into the cabin.

It was about 0400 by then. An Englishman came out of the cabin and warmly shook my hand in thanks. All seven of his crew were safe; it was a happy moment. Thierry and I were in the stern. We hugged each other fiercely: we had succeeded.

I had been lucky to have a worthy, robust boat that handled well and a supportive crew member like twenty-year-old Thierry. From the moment I took over the helm of the boat I knew I would succeed. Thierry had been doing all he could to sail *Lorelei* but under the circumstances a more delicate touch was needed. It was a question of not rushing into things or losing one's calm. Seven people were alive on that liferaft; they could have died of cold or drowned. But we saved them. We had had to be in a position of strength to save them otherwise we could have caused their deaths by a hasty manoeuvre.

With the seven castaways on board, either Thierry or Gerard took over the helm and we turned to head north without sail. Rollers occasionally broke over the hull but the boat remained stable. I went back into the cabin: I had slept only two or three hours since our departure. I had hoped that Thierry would stay at the helm for most of the Fastnet leg, but I was prevented from resting, first by the calm seas and then by the spinnaker runs with wind speeds of thirty knots and everyone in the cockpit.

The English navigator, Stuart Quarrie, was the last castaway to be taken on board. He had been laid on a bunk and covered up. Jacqueline, our ship's doctor, thought he would die; his nails were cyanosed and he shivered and trembled ceaselessly. He managed to tell us that his boat, *Griffin*, the new Class III of the English RORC, had turned over completely and gone down about two hours earlier. When it was righted it had been full of water and began to sink. The portholes, hatches and other openings were awash; the crew – who had been in their bunks – rushed to get into the liferaft. Only when Stuart told me that did I realise that his crew were not fishermen but, like us, they were competitors in the Fastnet race. He repeated time and again that, without us, he would have died of cold or by drowning. I knew now that Stuart was the navigator, but who was the skipper? There was no way of telling from the faces around me; all of them had a fixed look reflecting their shock at still being alive.

I realised that we were about a hundred miles from the English coast. I reassured Stuart that there was no question of the *Lorelei* continuing the race. I did not want to run before the storm with such enormous waves and in a heavily laden boat.

We had about a hundred litres of water in the bilges which we had taken on during the rescue; the companion way had been open and the washboard removed. The boat was resisting the bad weather marvellously. I got out the pump and started to get rid of the water; soon Marc relieved me of this duty. This was the only time that we used the pump to empty the boat. The cabin radio goniometer must have been hit by waves; it was no longer working either for direction purposes or for weather reports.

Stuart later continued his story. Their liferaft had turned over; the awning had not held on its mountings and the crew had found themselves in the sea with no idea where they were. The black of the liferaft made it difficult for them to reboard in the darkness, and without the awning, they were no longer sheltered. The trouble they had had getting back into the liferaft explained why several of them were sitting on the gunwales when we found them.

I had to prevent *Lorelei* drifting with the waves. I hoped that with an average speed of eight or nine knots we would reach the coast in ten hours. Moreover, the depression was lying on the east-west axis and moving towards the east and I would be left in the dangerous sector. Gerard was at the helm and first headed north. All of a sudden the boat pitched forward very heavily; the starboard side shook a lot but finally recovered. Stuart was worried about Gerard, but as I approached the companion way, Gerard told me to close it again and that all was going well as we turned to head south. Providence had prevented us carrying out the manoeuvre under sail. Using very little sail we turned south. I don't know how long it took; Gerard helmed for a long time without tiring, while *Lorelei* was incessantly battered by breakers.

Thierry relieved Gerard at the helm. The boat was awash at least twice. On the second occasion the compass had done a quarter turn and jammed. I took it to pieces, mended it and put it together again; at last we had a course to follow.

Since the rescue the anemometer had stuck at sixty knots – it could not go much further. It had been about fifteen hours and we seemed to be coming out of the bad weather zone. The wind dropped to fifty knots, sometimes to forty-five, and although it returned to fifty-five, it seemed calmer. Stuart was no longer trembling. It looked like we were over the worst.

At daybreak the next day I made tea and bread and butter with marmalade – for thirteen. Finally, I was able to drink my own cup of tea. The next thing I knew we were swamped by a wave. I was sitting on the engine cover with my feet fixed under the galley. I saw all the crockery shoot from port to starboard and then found myself with my head in the galley locker. It was a brief alarm. Soon we were heading north once more and everyone on board seemed well. Luckily, *Lorelei* does not have too much beam for her length. Something for which we were grateful.

We could not remain in our confined shelter for more than ten minutes at a time as the smell down below had become overpowering. The English crew – and indeed my own crew – were continually asking for the bucket to be sick. I had never been seasick before but I found myself in the same predicament. Towards 1700 I moved a spinnaker bag. Stuart asked me anxiously if I was going to use it. I reassured him and prepared the stormsail which we then hoisted; after sailing for two or three hours we ran up the mainsail. When it had first been hauled down, the sail had suffered some damage and so I hoisted a replacement sail with three reefs.

We set our course for Scilly. At last we had some respite: the wind dropped to forty or forty-five knots. It dropped again and we set the No. 2 sail. On Wednesday morning we passed between Scilly and the English coast; we were using the mainsail, under the spinnaker and in sunshine. At 1100 everyone was on deck. I emptied *Lorelei* of all her fittings and spent an hour cleaning the cabin. Gerard and Marc had prepared an extraordinary (for a boat) meal: tomato salad (Bordeaux style); chicken; sautéd veal with carrots; fruit; cheese, and dessert, complemented with a fine Médoc.

The English were delighted by our French cuisine and began to chat and laugh and help us tend the spinnaker sheet. I think one of them even offered to sail the boat. In the evening we crossed the finishing line at about 2300. The English crew was bedded down below. We had lent them clothes, but as far as we knew they had neither money nor papers.

They woke us at 1000. Somehow they had managed to find money to buy white wine and cigarettes with which to celebrate their return. They finally went home to their families and the adventure was over.

Some personal reflections

The way that we had ridden out the bad weather might seem a paradox. However, the success of the rescue confirmed that I had chosen the right boat. I had worked for hundreds of hours in *Lorelei*, I knew every detail of her cabin and deck and I had enormous confidence in her. Her frigate form had helped the hull resist the impact of the breakers. There were no right-angled structures topside – only the curves designed by the architect of She 36. Olin Stephens has, without doubt, contributed more than anyone to cruiser/racer design. Only the She or the Swan are as well constructed.

Thirteen of us lived on *Lorelei*; a feat few boats of her size could have managed without damage. Olin Stephens' design enabled us to save seven Englishmen.

POSTSCRIPT

by Clare Francis

At sea only a very thin line can be drawn between safety and fool-hardiness, between keeping a boat within her limits and over-extending her. Some would say that nowadays this line has to be crossed to win a race, others argue that experienced crews can push thoroughbred racing yachts to the highest limits of safety. The 1979 Fastnet Race brought these arguments to the fore.

The Fastnet Race Report tries to sort through the multitude of facts and opinions that are available and to determine what lessons can be learned. Its reasoning and conclusions are considered, balanced and fair; and yet in the most important area of all — recommendations — it is very cautious, and as many lessons can be learnt from the body of the Report as from the recommendations themselves.

Quite rightly the Report highlights the advisability of staying with the boat unless it actually sinks. (Of the twenty-four yachts abandoned, only four sank and a fifth sank under tow.) Seven lives were lost from liferafts or while being rescued from liferafts; several liferafts disintegrated or capsized — a sobering thought for anyone who sails offshore. Liferaft manufacturers have been asked to look at design.

The other disturbing area concerning equipment was the failure of harnesses. Six lives are believed lost as a result of clips or harnesses breaking or of them being attached to weak points like guard-rails. The need for specific harness-attachment points is emphasised.

Hull designs which are inclined to roll right over (wide-beamed boats) are vaguely criticised but considered outside the scope of the report because the matter is so technical. Cockpits which do not drain adequately, weak rudders, lack of watertight companionways, and stowage were also found to be inadequate.

However, the main blame for the disaster is laid on the sea itself, although the Report does admit that the conditions were not exceptional. Here I believe that the main issue is understated; many skippers and boats were simply not prepared to meet weather that a yacht on long passage would expect to meet. Thus many Fastnet competitors failed to carry such basic equipment as bolt-cutters, buckets for bailing out, washboard fixings, adequate hand-rails, and batter- and cooker-retainers which hold beyond 90° inversion.

The Report finds a slight correlation between experience and safety — as would be expected — and notes two tactics that seemed to pay:

1 Crews who sheltered below, leaving only helmsmen plus perhaps one other on deck, avoided the effects of exposure and were therefore more effective throughout the storm.

2 Active rather than passive tactics seemed to be successful.

This second point is very much understated. There is strong evidence to show that those who kept their boats moving – either up or downwind – fared much better than those who lay a-hull or hove-to. Many were unable to make effective weathering because they lacked a third, deep reef in their mainsails (racing sail-makers do not put them in) or did not possess a trisail (the majority of the fleet did not). Trisails are now to become compulsory. Those who were knocked down were generally sailing slowly, or drifting. Those who experimented found that a reasonable speed was much safer (a conclusion that most skippers in the Round the World Race reached). The reasons are fairly obvious: manoeuvrability and ability to take waves at a favourable angle.

The need for communications was another recommendation. But until the DoT relax their ridiculously high standards for MF transmitters, it is unlikely ordinary yachtsmen can fit these sets because of cost and space. VHF Channel 16 was grossly overcrowded during the storm and therefore largely unworkable.

In conclusion, the Report is well worth studying and many lessons can be learnt. In particular, there is a lesson we have to learn time and time again: never underestimate the sea.

THE MEETS

The Beaulieu River Meet
by Maldwin Drummond

The anchorage under Gull Island is a place of many moods, every expression of which has been shown to the Club during the annual meet. This year the estuary was warm and welcoming; there was a tinge of sadness, however, as the Commodore, Ronnie Andrews, was prevented from attending by illness. Rosemary, his wife, sailed through the fleet aboard David Kimber's inflatable catamaran, giving life to her short verse:

> *Sailing down the river in David's latest craft,*
> *Rubber dinghy with a sail, a plate, and rudder aft.*
> *I covered the casing over, lest the whale decide to spray*
> *And leisurely we toured the fleet in a right and proper way.*

John Power, the Vice, and Scrap Batten, the Rear Commodores, entertained and encouraged the fleet. A launch was provided for the first time by the Harbour-Master, which would have proved invaluable had not neaps and the weather smiled on transport in anything larger than an oyster shell.

YACHTS ATTENDING

Abigail III, Aceca, Anahita III, Acquest, Asterie, Bella Donna, Blue Dolphin of Wight, Blue Shank, Blue Vinney, Bow Bells, Bowstring, Brigus, Candide, Capelan, Chal, Corruna, Cymbeline, Cyn III, Decibel, Dorado, Dreolin, Dyarchy, Fair Joanda, Farida, Firecrest, Frisk, Fubbs, Guiding Star, Gulliver G, Harkaway, Havfruen IV, Hažana, Ivory Gull, Janet Mor, Juno, Keeshond, Keryl, Knotty, La Snook, Leonie, Marlin, Mary Helen, Micia, Minimosh, Moonstar, Morning Sky, Mowgli, New Melody, Osiris, Palafox 2, Pas Seul, Penny Royal, Phalarope, Quanto II, Respect, Robertson's Golly, Rosalind, Royal Flush, Salanna, Sausalito, Sequel, Sharavoge, Silver Sonnet, Stag, Starwalker, Ste Anne d' Auray, Styria, Susmar, Tamare, Wandering Moon, Water Music III, Wishart.

The East Coast Meet

by J.T. Edwards

The 1979 East Coast Meet was held on 19th May at the Suffolk Yacht Club on the Orwell.

Tim Hall made splendid arrangements at a new anchorage — lying alongside 'marine' pontoons. It was far more convenient for visiting than the East Coast anchorages, with their fast-running tides, that we have used for the last twenty-five years.

An excellent dinner was served in the old lightship of the Haven Ports Yacht Club. More members and more boats than in the past few years were able to enjoy a most pleasant weekend. The locals were proud that the Vice-Commodore and Caroline had sailed from the Solent in horrible weather to be with us, Trevor Wilkinson did not come on his sailboard and several members were unable to come in their own boats because of foul weather.

YACHTS ATTENDING

Affray, Blue Shore, Coriander, Martha McGilda, Penny Royal, Sirius of Avon.

The Irish Cruising Club's Fiftieth Anniversary and the Golden Jubilee Cruise of South-west Ireland

by Hugh Davies

A cruise-in-company is not everyone's cup of tea. There are those that fear that a week or so of roistering, party-going and general merry-making will rot their souls and blemish the purity of their cruising. However, there were enough gregarious RCC members prepared to tolerate the hazards associated with such junkets: forty-eight yachts attended all or part of the Irish Cruising Club's fiftieth anniversary Golden Jubilee Cruise of south-west Ireland. The fleet was composed of yachts from the Irish Cruising Club, the Royal Cork Yacht Club, the Royal Cruising Club, the Clyde Cruising Club, and the Cruising Club of America. (Some skippers were members of as many as three participating clubs.) There was a total of over 150 vessels.

On arrival, visitors reported to the ICC reception caravan, staffed by John Minchin and Rosemary Cagney of the RCYC, and were issued with an up-dated programme; a list of yachts, owners and guests; name badges; tickets for each of the four parties that were held around the course; a copy of *The Guiness Book of Records*; information on local amenities, and other useful items.

The night before the cruise a party was held in the Majorca Ballroom. The main feature of the ballroom was the large open fire in the centre of the dance-floor, the smoke and fumes of which escaped through the chimney by means of a massive hood. The evening was warm, the fire was very hot and the management did great business in the bars. We also enjoyed the spirited performance of an Irish bag-pipe band.

The Irish Prime Minister, Mr. Jack Lynch, was to have attended but he was kept away by business. However, we were delighted that Mrs. Lynch was able to be with us.

At 1130 the next morning, Saturday 21st July, the fleet headed west for Castletownshend, the venue for the RCC/CCC party on the 23rd. Some of the fleet went straight to Castletownshend, a few of us decided to visit Glandore. As there was a northerly wind, we chose to lay off Glandore, quite close to the jetty and in calm water. Our walk ashore the next morning confirmed that Glandore is beautifully un-spoiled.

On Monday the 23rd, a bright chilly day, we motor-sailed lazily to Castletownshend. In the evening the RCC/CCC party was held in the lovely grounds of Drishane House – a magnificent venue.

Ray Fielding, in *Spellbound*, had suggested a trip to Barloga and on to Skull via the passage leading north out of Baltimore harbour. So, the following morning, we were very glad to join the party of nine boats: five American, three Irish and one British. Lough Hyne connects with Barloge cove and the sea by a narrow channel of some two or three hundred yards in length. The tide was ebbing and the current was strong, so we rowed ashore and walked up the short waterway, which – according to ICC sailing directions – 'becomes a scour at half tide'; there are also quite fierce rapids close to the top. The Lough is enchanting and well worth a visit. Other people, more energetic than ourselves, had portaged their dinghy to the Lough and shot the rapids on the way back.

From Barloge, Ray led his little flotilla into Roaring Water Bay by way of the inner passage between Span Point and Carrigthrue and inside the Kedges. From there we proceeded to Baltimore harbour and through the passage between Spanish Island and The Sound, Quarantine and Sandy Islands, anchoring for lunch just north of Woman Rock. The next part of our journey was out into Roaring Water via Corrignamoe, south of Frolic Point, and through the channel between Goose and Rabbit Islands, across the bay and inside Horse and Castle Islands. We anchored in Skull harbour at 1640.

On Wednesday the 25th, there was little wind for our modest, slightly murky passage to Crookhaven in company with *Wandering Moon*. *Osiris's* log, however, records a cheerful evening spent in the local pub.

At 0900 the next morning we were on our way again with several other yachts. (It was on Thursday that ten crews landed on the Fastnet Rock, a rare opportunity.) We rounded Mizen Head and enjoyed a gentle reach across Dunmanus and Bantry Bays into Castletownberehaven.

That evening we attended the CCA party at the Cametringane Hotel. John Guinness and Peter Comstock, commodores of the ICC and CCA, proposed to form a 'sunflower' in Adrigole the next day, some eight miles to the east. A sunflower is a circle of yachts radiating like petals from a central point, bows pointing outwards and sterns into the centre. This great floral decoration was arranged in Adrigole the following afternoon. It was set up by Porter Schutt, anchoring *Deramore* fore and aft; he was followed by John Guinness in *Deerhound*, anchoring downwind and opposite *Deramore*. These first two yachts, facing in opposite directions, formed the diameter of a circle. The sunflower was completed by other yachts filling in the halves of the circle. Every third yacht anchored into position, tying up to the vessels on either side. There was a total of seventy yachts.

When we finally upped anchor for the demanding sail to Glengariff at the head of Bantry Bay, some people were worried that there would be a great dogfish breakfast and ensnarled anchors and cables. Everyone departed in good order, however, a tribute to the sunflower organisers and the seamanship of those present. The petals blew away elegantly.

On Saturday, 28th July, we sailed to Glengariff, where the ICC was founded fifty years ago. The ICC sailing directions tell us that Glengariff is called the Madeira of Ireland because of its mild climate.

The Irish President, Dr. Patrick Hillary, attended a reception on board the Irish naval vessel, *L.E. Emer*, to which the flag officers of the attending clubs were invited. In the afternoon a tea party was held aboard the Irish Lights Tender *Granuaile*, and Garnish Island, with its enchanting formal and informal gardens, was the venue for the ICC party. There was an impressive exchange of gifts between the clubs, and speeches from the flag officers presenting them.

After a day of rest in Glengariff we returned to Castletown in a strong south-south-west wind, with poor visibility and driving rain and listened with sympathy to a radio conversation between *Deerhound* and a number of other yachts that were assisting *Adele*, owned by Bunny Burnes (CCA), which had lost her mast. We later learned that *Deerhound* accompanied *Adele* into Adrigole, where both crews spent many hours cutting the mast into stowable lengths and cleaning up the mess. *Adele* was later able to proceed under her own power to Crosshaven, where she awaits refitting.

The fleet eventually dispersed, some like *Osiris* homeward bound, while others took advantage of a wonderful opportunity to explore the west coast of Ireland. Apparently a number of crews landed on Skellig Michael. It was a memorable cruise and a fitting tribute to the Golden Jubilee of the ICC.

YACHTS ATTENDING

Aeolian, Akarana, Arctic Skua, Autonomy, Battle Royal, Blue Dolphin of Wight, Blueshank, Brigus, Caressa, Catonga, Confidante, Corofin, Cyn III, Deerhound, Deramore, Dreolin, Dyarchy, Endeavour, Fiasco of Ashton, Gloriana, Helen of Howth, Jarema, Jubilee, Juno, Keeshond, Klompen, Lumpy Custard, Meermin, Morning Sky, Musketeer, Norfolk Nip, Osiris, Pampa Mia, Penny Royal, Phalarope, Quanto II, Quicksilver, Sausalito, Sharavoge, Spellbound, Tetra, Thumper, Troubadour, Velsia, Verve, Wandering Moon, Wester Till, Yeong.

The Junior Meet

by Andrew J.S. O'Grady

The Junior Meet was held in the last weekend in September at East Head in Chichester Harbour. Once again the weather-god looked kindly upon us: even if we saw little sun, at least we had no rain. Those who came from the Solent enjoyed a wet beat into a strong easterly wind with an east-going tide making for a fair chop; some found this hair-raising, others plain nauseating. Your correspondent's vessel fell off a large wave and sprang a plank in the bow and arrived with the pump hard at work and the crew somewhat downcast.

Harkaway and *Brigus* arrived at lunch-time with *Blueshank, Penny Royal* and *Seawing* arriving later in the afternoon. We collected a large pile of driftwood for the fire, carefully avoiding any pieces which could have belonged to any of the sand-breaks on the beach. This policy paid off: when the fire was lit, a fully uniformed policeman arrived off a patrolling launch to bring the 'No bonfires' notice to the attention of the Cadet Members' Secretary. Luckily Kit was able to point out the complete absence of any illicit wood in our pile and so we were let off the hook. The rest of the evening was spent happily eating, singing and drinking around the roaring fire.

On Sunday morning *Blueshank* and *Seawing* left early and *Harkaway* took to the beach for repairs. Kit and Penny Power, who had so ably organised the occasion, provided the remaining crews with lunch and the fleet broke up in the afternoon after a memorable meet.

CRUISING ACTIVITIES

1. **The UK** (including the Channel Islands and the Scillies)

   Abigail III. Arvor III, Black Velvet, Brigus, Caressa, Clairvoyance, Filette, Foggy Dew, Harkaway, Hannah Penn, Gavotte II, Gloriana, Isle of Huney, Keryl, Leonie, Maggie May, Matawa, Micia, Ondine of Dorset, Quanto II, Sausalito, Stroller, Windflower.

2. **The West Coast of Scotland**

   Foggy Dew, Fubbs, Gloriana, Matawa, Quicksilver, Suhaili.

3. **Ireland**

   Autonomy, Blue Shank, Brigus, Caressa, Confidante, Dyarchy, Fair Joanda, Morning Sky, Penny Royal, Phalarope, Quanto II, Quicksilver, Sausalito, Sharavoge, Starwalker, Stroller, Wandering Moon, Warrior Shamaal, Yeong.

4. **Norway** (the West Coast)

   Janet Mor

5. **Skagerrack, Kattegat and Denmark**

   Foggy Dew, Lorbas, Quicksilver.

6. **East Denmark**

   Watchdog of Wareham.

7. **The Low Countries, Germany and the Inland Waterways**

   Cheemaun, Decibel, Lorbas, Naseby, Pentina II.

8. **Normandy** (Calais to St. Malo)

   Clairvoyance, Confidante, Decibel, Filette, Isle of Huney, Leonie, Warrior Shamaal.

141

9. **North Brittany**

   Abigail III, Acquest, Bow Bells, Blue Vinny, Caressa, Chal, Clairvoyance, Felicity Al, Filette, Gavotte II, Hannah Penn, Harkaway, Havfruen, Knotty, La Snook, Leonie, Matawa, Morning Sky, Palafox 2, Offbeat III, Ondine of Dorset, Sausalito, Stag, Starwalker, Warrior Shamaal.

10. **North Biscay** (Brest to La Rochelle)

    Acquest, Blue Vinny, Chal, Felicity Al, Filette, Gavotte II, Jolie Brise, La Snook, Matawa, Micia, Ondine of Dorset, Offbeat III, Palafox 2, Quicksilver, Saecwen, Sausalito, Scalza, Stag.

11. **South Biscay** (La Rochelle to the Spanish Coast)

    Jolie Brise, Scalza.

12. **North-west Spain**

    Acquest, Autonomy, Gloriana, Jolie Brise, Quicksilver, Saecwen, Watermusic III.

13. **The West Mediterranean** (the rest of Spain, the Balearics, the Tyrrhenian Sea, Malta and North Africa)

    Acquest, Gloriana, Quicksilver, Saecwen, Scalza, Watermusic III.

14. **The East Mediterranean** (the Aegean and Ionian Sea, Turkey and the Levant)

    Lutra II, Maridadi, Return, Thyateira.

15. **The Atlantic and Caribbean** (including the West Coast of the Americas and Canada)

    Aglaia, Dyarchy, Offbeat III, Wanderer IV, Whisper.

16. **The High Latitudes, the Arctic and Antarctic** (including Greenland, the North-West Passage and Jane Mayen in the North, the Falkland Islands and South Georgia)

    Capricornus, Forrest.

17. **Events**

    Autonomy, Sarais Marais (the Fastnet Race).

18. **Technical Notes**

    Autonomy.

BOOK REVIEWS

by Maldwin Drummond

The Sea Bird by Rozelle Raynes, published by Springwood Books (£6.95)

Rozelle Raynes describes her love for the sea and where that passion led her. Some authors look back on a sea-water life with closing eyes, as though tired from looking permanently to weather; *Sea Bird* has a down-wind sparkle about it. Rozelle Raynes' love of salt air is still as bright as when, dressed in a long nighty, she first looked expectantly from her parents' Victorian house in South Kensington towards the Thames, responding to the sound of a tug's fog-horn.

At seventeen, she joined the WRNS and later worked aboard a 100-ton cutter, before taking to the sea — sometimes single-handed — in her Folkboat. Rozelle now has her yachtmaster's certificate and is a member of the committee of the Royal Cruising Club. Her progress, so well recorded, is well worth following.

A Thirst for the Sea, introduced and edited by Hugh and Robin Popham, published by Stanford Maritime (£6.95)

Erskine Childers won the Royal Cruising Club's Admiral de Horsey Cup in 1896 for his contribution 'to the Club the work which shall be adjudged, under these rules, to furnish the most useful information for the purposes of the Club'. He was elected to the Committee in 1901.

Hugh Popham and his wife Robin, both experienced sailors, trace the development of Erskine Childers' 'thirst for the sea' from his first yacht *Shulah* through to *Asgard*. Other yachts include *Marguerite* (his experience aboard which led to the de Horsey Cup) and *Vixen*, whose cruise of 1897 was to form the canvas on which he so skilfully embroidered the finest sailing novel ever written, *The Riddle of the Sands*, first published in 1903.

A Thirst for the Sea is particularly absorbing, for it is a collection taken from all that Childers wrote about the sea. There are pages from his actual logs and these are supplemented by articles that he wrote for *The Yachting Monthly* and *The Times*. If there are two books that should be in every serious cruising man's bookshelf, afloat and ashore, *The Riddle of the Sands* is one and *A Thirst for the Sea* is its close companion.

143

Saga of Direction by Charles H. Vilas, published by Seven Seas Press ($12.95)

'Carl' Vilas needs no introduction to members of the Royal Cruising Club in this centenary year; he is the editor of the *Cruising Club of America News*, which brought out the joint edition with the Royal Cruising Club in celebration of our first hundred years at sea.

In this beautifully produced saga he lovingly describes every detail of his yacht *Direction*. He has been her master since 1946, for thirty-four of her fifty-four years. *Direction* is a scaled-down version of a Colin Archer Redningskoite, or rescue boat. She became famous for her cruise to Greenland and for being wrecked there in 1929, the year of her birth. The famous artist, Rockwell Kent, recorded the experience in the best-seller *N by E*.

Carl's ideas and practical hints round off the preceding adventures. He shows the reader how much the amateur sailor owes to designers like Colin Archer, who made small vessels the basis of a home at sea. Carl Vilas records a lifetime of experience and practical improvement in a way that is both valuable, good to look at and easy to understand.

Colin Archer and the Seaworthy Double Ender by John Leather, published by Stanford Maritime (£9.95)

John Leather has made a name for himself amongst cruising yachtsmen. He has a seaman's eye — rare among yachting writers — and can distinguish what is right among a host of wrongs. It is, therefore, particularly fortunate, although not surprising, that he has looked, and looked well, at the work of Colin Archer and those who followed his ideas. The book is a testimony to an artist who really understood how to design and build a vessel that could respond to extreme conditions. Colin Archer (1832-1921) took the traditional Norwegian double ender, which developed slowly from Viking times and turned it into a rescue boat that was capable of saving the lives of Norwegian fishermen under sail alone, off a dangerous coast and in all weathers.

Erskine Childers' *Asgard* came from Archer's board and Carl Vilas' *Direction* was scaled down from Archer's actual lines by M.H. Miner of New York. *Teddy* was a 40-footer, designed and built by Archer as a pilot boat for Larvik in 1890. She became famous through Erling Tamb's honeymoon cruise to the South Seas and his book about it, *The Cruise of the Teddy*.

Oeger, another child of Archer, was built as a yacht by Jensen of Porsgrunn for an Englishman called Haig. She was bought by Ralph Stock, a soldier, for £300 during the First World War. He fitted her out with the help of his profits from trawling and sailed to the Society Islands. His book, *The Cruise of a Dreamship — On Dreams and How to Realise Them*, convinced a wide public of the ability of Archer's ships. John Leather has gathered together this genius and presents a particularly readable and well illustrated tribute to a designer of singular talent.

144

OBITUARIES

J.F. Dibben

Jack Dibben died in July 1979, only a week after his wife, Molly. I feel that her name should be linked with his in this short appreciation. They had sailed together since their marriage before the war (during which Jack served in the RNVR). Their first boat was *Carol*, and after the war – usually with one or more of their three sons – they sailed in *Half Pint, Maxine, Moshulu* and finally, *Palinode*. Jack and Molly often took friends with them on their cruises but they are perhaps best remembered as the parents of a happy sailing family.

For many years Jack's disability prevented him from walking more than a few yards at a time, but he refused to accept the restrictions of age or infirmity. He never reminisced: there was always a future and his watchword was 'over the bow'. He was normally of a quiet, relaxed disposition, but when cruising he was restless: having arrived, his next objective was to depart.

Jack was not a gregarious person but he was always welcoming and hospitable in his own boat. He and Molly are sadly missed by their family and friends.

DEB

Professor John Francis

John Francis died suddenly last March at the age of fifty-eight. He began sailing as a boy during the 1930s in dinghies and small open boats at Shoreham. He took his degree in 1940 and became a Lieutenant RNVR, working for most of the war on the development of various weapons and devices, notably the Hedgehog anti-submarine mortar.

Immediately after the war he and his brother were joint owners of a number of small cruisers: *Eve*, an old Luke gaff cutter; *Josephine*, a Tumlaren, and *Malista*, a Folkboat. In these boats he cruised the South Coast and Britanny.

In 1968 he bought *Seafire*, a Lymington Slipway four-tonner and on being appointed to the Chair of Municipal Engineering at Manchester, he moved his sailing operations to the Clyde with *Fae* and later *Shona of Melford*. With his wife, Sheila (a botanist specialising in mycology), he cruised extensively in Scottish waters. He continued to do so after his appointment to the Chair of Hydraulics at the Imperial College of Science and Technology in London, which he held at the time of his death.

He was elected to the RCC in 1968. His presence will be missed, particularly by those whom he introduced as members.

CGF and **MJG**

145

Dr. William Murray Mackinlay

Willie Mackinlay was amongst that band of Scottish yachting pioneers who created between the two World Wars much of what is taken for granted today. Along with a number of colleagues, he was responsible for introducing the Dragon Class from Norway to Scottish waters. Those magnificent little boats not only provided excellent racing but were also cruised extensively. The class then went on to International and Olympic recognition. Willie and his colleagues were behind the presentation of the Dragon Gold Cup, still an annual international competition in European waters.

He held many positions in yachting administration until the late seventies. Among the appointments he held were Honorary Secretary of the Royal Western Yacht Club of Scotland, Chairman of The Clyde Yacht Clubs' Association, and positions in the Royal Yachting Association; he was also involved with the International Yacht Racing Union. He recently was Vice-Admiral of the Mudhook Yacht Club and as a Member of the Royal Yacht Squadron served on many Protest Committees and Juries at Cowes Week throughout the last decade.

However, Willie was a cruising man at heart and throughout his sailing days owned several magnificent boats. Notable among these are the eight-metre *Margaret*, with which he cruised extensively on the West Coast of Scotland, and the Herreshoff cutter, *Neith*, which is now to be preserved in a Maritime Museum in America.

After the sale of *Neith* many years ago, Willie chartered regularly and cruised on the West Coast of Scotland. As an Honorary Member of Clyde Cruising Club, he chaired the log-judging panel for twelve years. He always expressed a keen interest in young people and presented an annual prize for the best junior log of the season.

Willie was also involved in public life in Glasgow and the West Coast of Scotland for which he was decorated with the OBE and subsequently the CBE. He was made an Honorary Doctor of Law by the University of Glasgow and served as a Justice of the Peace.

AGT

Dr. A.G.C. Taylor

'Pompey' Taylor was the son of a general and was originally destined for the army. However, he went instead to St. Thomas's Hospital as a mature student.

In 1927, while still a student and with the help of his Aunt Nora's will, he bought *Charity*, an eight-ton straight-stemmed gaff cutter, and based her on the East Coast. In 1928 he was elected to the RCC. I suspect – although I was too young to witness – that Pompey brought a medical student's high spirits to cruising. East about round the British Isles, while waiting for the weather in a North Scottish harbour, he was involved in the abduction of a publican's hat. And so, he said, he had crossed the Pentland Firth before he had time to be frightened.

During a research appointment at Middlesex Hospital, he met Mary. He and *Charity* must have been an engaging pair: she and Pompey were married.

As Director of Radio Therapy for Southern Hampshire and living at Sopp's Farm there must have been little time for cruising: *Charity* was sold. He owned a series of small racing boats, based at Cracknor Hard or Hamble and incorporated Aunt Nora's name in them all.

Pompey and Mary returned to cruising in 1963 with *Tetranora*, mainly in the Channel and Brittany and Biscay. In 1967 they bought *Pentanora*, a Nicholson 38. Pompey celebrated his seventy-fifth birthday in the Scillies, during a short cruise-in-company.

Pompey and Mary often cruised with John and Irene Purvis; when John died suddenly in 1977 they could no longer manage. *Pentanora* was sold.

Mary died in her sleep at her beloved Sopp's Farm in 1978; Pompey died less than a month later.

PEGB

Tilman

No passage of Magellan Strait should be undertaken without reading Tilman's *Mischief in Patagonia*. Newbold Smith of the CCA says the same about Spitzbergen, where, in *Baroque*, Tilman 'sailed further north at 80° 4' than any yachtsman in history'. That Tilman's objectives have been beyond the reach of most was recognised by the CCA when he was awarded the Blue Water Medal for his 'Voyage of *Exploration* to Patagonia' (my italics). Tilman's adventures under sail have been of a different nature from ordinary long-distance ocean cruising. No doubt this accounts for his name being so little known in comparison to that of his fellow RCC member, Sir Francis Chichester, for example.

It is ironic that the first love of this great seaman was the mountains. Indeed, he once told me that an Antarctic voyage I was contemplating was pointless unless it culminated in a climb. High Himalaya, the Polar pack, the sword and the pen; it is hardly credible that one man could have left his mark with such distinction and in so many fields.

Tilman was born in 1898; he served in the Royal Artillery on the Western Front, where he won the MC and Bar. After the War he took up coffee planting in Kenya from where he took his home leave by bicycling three thousand miles across Africa, living on mealie meal and bananas. It was this feat that induced Eric Shipton to seek him

147

out and introduce him to mountaineering; their brilliant *tour de force* on Mount Kenya was his 'blooding'. There followed ascents in Sinkiang, Afghanistan and the Himalayas, including Nanda Devi in 1936, and the leadership of the Everest Expedition in 1938.

In 1939 Major Tilman joined the Royal Artillery in France and served in Syria, Iraq, the Western Desert, and Tunisia. He was dropped by parachute to fight with Albanian and then Italian partisans and so became a guerilla fighter. During the latter campaign Tilman had the affrontery to establish his HQ on the top floor of the Gestapo building in Belluno. When inevitably the hunt was up, his partisans smuggled him out in a coffin and buried him in the cemetery, resurrecting him late that night. Not inappropriately, he was made a freeman of the city of Belluno and awarded the DSO.

After the war Tilman made further climbs in Sinkiang and Nepal and then took up sailing as a means of reaching remote, virgin mountains. Thus began the sagas of *Mischief, Sea Breeze, Baroque, Patanella* and *En Avant.* He was eighty when he set out on his last voyage.

Tilman's fourteen books are far more than cruising logs or tales of alpine adventure. His dry humour, his sense of fellowship with explorers of the past and the breadth of his scholarship (he was made LLD by the University of St. Andrews) enable his works to transcend the bounds of their immediate subject matter.

Despite his extraordinary achievements Tilman was a modest man. In 1946 he ignored his magnificent war record and quoted from *The Ancient Mariner* to express his feelings at surviving the holocaust:

The many men, so beautiful!
And they all dead did lie:
And thousand thousand slimy things
Live on; and so did I.

I will remember his pleasure after a Welsh climb. 'Was that *really* a "severe" we did? We can't be quite past it then!' There was also his genuine surprise at finding his name – together with that of Hillary – on the ceiling of the climbers' pub at Pen-y-Gwryd. 'They still remember me,' he said.

Tilman was always patient and helpful with beginners if he knew their interest was genuine. However, his patience did not exclude well deserved scathing criticism. But in conversation or writing, no matter how critical he was of the pikers who made up a proportion of his crews, he was invariably hardest of all on himself and stressed his own mistakes.

It is not easy to comprehend the full measure of Tilman's seamanship. Each one of his voyages was an outstanding expedition; any one of them would have placed his name among the immortals. The loss of *Mischief* off Jan Mayen and *Sea Breeze* off East Greenland in no way detracts from his remarkable record. His achievements were due solely to his superb seamanship. Only one man was lost during all Tilman's expeditions, which puts him on a par with Shackleton. Some episodes are mind-boggling; for instance, the penetration of Lancaster Sound in the frail *Mischief* a week ahead of the season's first ice-strengthened supply ship – a triumph of ice pilotage.

Crew difficulties plagued many of Tilman's expeditions, largely because there were simply not enough first-class men to keep up with his long annual voyages. Like Woodes Rogers and Dampier, who, during the seventeenth century, took the Manila Galleon with a crew of 'Jail birds and Chelsea Pensioners' and needed only three days to teach them seamanship and bring them to discipline', Tilman expected much of his crews and the fears and doubts of modern imaginative young men were hard for Tilman to comprehend or to handle and he certainly underestimated the stamina and suitability of women. 'I regret that some of my crew adopted the unseamanlike habit of wearing gloves at the helm,' Tilman once admitted disapprovingly during an Arctic cruise. Food was spartan but plentiful; Tilman believed in adequate 'belly timber'. He demanded a good deal of courage and toughness on his voyages and it is only natural that some crew should fall by the wayside.

However, when men of a higher calibre made up the party it was a different story. They considered it a privilege to sail under one of the world's great seamen. Proctor, later lost off the Solomons during a single-handed circumnavigation in a *Trekka*, was one such. All of his crew – Deacock, Putt, Budd and the rest – were distinguished mountaineers and Polar explorers in their own right.

Major Tilman added lustre to British arms and to British letters; his mountaineering skills and his seamanship are unforgettable. The best tribute to him is that others are following where he led. Perhaps this is Bill Tilman's proudest legacy.

DL